TREKKING MUNICH TO VENICE

THE TRAUMPFAD, 'DREAM WAY', A CLASSIC TREK
ACROSS THE EASTERN ALPS

About the Author

John Hayes is a retired management consultant with degrees from Liverpool University and University College London. Immediately after finishing work in 2011 he embarked on an epic 5000km trek across Europe, walking from Tarifa in Spain to Budapest. John has written for numerous walking and trekking magazines.

Having walked various parts of the Munich to Venice route on different visits to the Alps John, with his wife Christine, embarked on his first through walk in 2014 returning again in 2015 to complete additional research.

Other Cicerone guides by the author
Spain's Sendero Histórico: The GR1

TREKKING MUNICH TO VENICE

THE TRAUMPFAD, 'DREAM WAY', A CLASSIC TREK ACROSS THE EASTERN ALPS

by John Hayes

2 POLICE SQUARE, MILNTHORPE, CUMBRIA LA7 7PY
www.cicerone.co.uk

Printed by KHL Printing, Singapore
A catalogue record for this book is available from the British Library.
All photographs are by the author unless otherwise stated.

Route mapping by Lovell Johns www.lovelljohns.com
Contains OpenStreetMap.org data © OpenStreetMap
contributors, CC-BY-SA. NASA relief data courtesy of ESRI

Acknowledgments

Thanks to Max and Frances Harre for testing an early version of the route description in 2015. Some of their photographs have been included in this guide.

Updates to this Guide

While every effort is made by our authors to ensure the accuracy of guidebooks as they go to print, changes can occur during the lifetime of an edition. Any updates that we know of for this guide will be on the Cicerone website (www.cicerone.co.uk/804/updates), so please check before planning your trip. We also advise that you check information about such things as transport, accommodation and shops locally. Even rights of way can be altered over time.

The route maps in this guide are derived from publicly available data, databases and crowd-sourced data. As such they have not been through the detailed checking procedures that would generally be applied to a published map from an official mapping agency, although we have reviewed them closely in the light of local knowledge as part of the preparation of this guide.

We are always grateful for information about any discrepancies between a guidebook and the facts on the ground, sent by email to updates@cicerone.co.uk or by post to Cicerone, 2 Police Square, Milnthorpe LA7 7PY, United Kingdom.

Front cover: Approaching the Kaserer Shartl (Stage 11B)

CONTENTS

Mountain Safety

Every mountain walk has its dangers, and the trek, described in this guidebook is no exception. All who walk or climb in the mountains should recognise this and take responsibility for themselves and their companions along the way. The author and publisher have made every effort to ensure that the information contained in this guide was correct when it went to press, but they cannot accept responsibility for any loss, injury or inconvenience sustained by any person using this book.

International Distress Signal *(emergency only)*
Six blasts on a whistle (and flashes with a torch after dark) spaced evenly for one minute, followed by a minute's pause. Repeat until an answer is received. The response is three signals per minute followed by a minute's pause.

Helicopter Rescue
The following signals are used to communicate with a helicopter:

Help needed:
raise both arms
above head to
form a 'Y'

Help not needed:
raise one arm
above head, extend
other arm downward

Emergency telephone numbers
The emergency telephone number for all Europe is 112

Official national weather services
Germany – Deutcher Wetterdienst www.dwd.de
Austria – Zentralanstalt für Meteorologie und Geodynamik www.zamg.ac
Italy – Meteo Aeronautica www.meteoam.it

Note Mountain rescue can be very expensive – be adequately insured.

Symbols used on route maps

～	route
▬ ▬ ▬	alternative route
Ⓢ	start point
Ⓕ	finish point
Ⓢ	alternative start
Ⓕ	alternative finish
❯	direction of route
	glacier
	woodland
	urban areas
	regional border
	international border
▬■▬	station/railway
▲	peak
⬆	hotel
⬆⬆	manned/unmanned hostel
⚓	campsite
🍴	restaurant
■	building
♦ †	chapel/cross
✚	monastery
🏰	castle
≍	bridge
)(	pass
⬅❶	junction

Relief
in metres

3200–3400	
3000–3200	
2800–3000	
2600–2800	
2400–2600	
2200–2400	
2000–2200	
1800–2000	
1600–1800	
1400–1600	
1200–1400	
1000–1200	
800–1000	
600–800	
400–600	
200–400	
0–200	

SCALE: 1:100,000

0 kilometres   1   2

0 miles   1

Contour lines are drawn at 50m intervals and highlighted at 200m intervals.

GPX files

GPX files for all routes can be downloaded free at www.cicerone.co.uk/804/GPX.

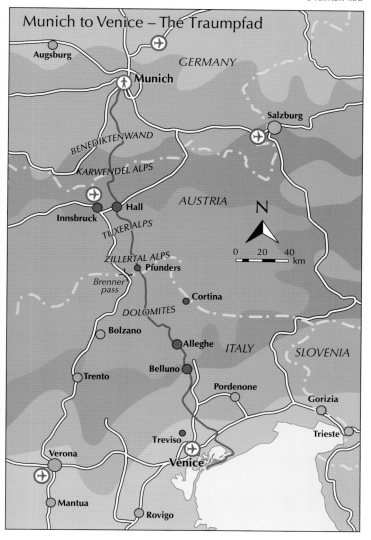

Munich to Venice – The Traumpfad

OVERVIEW MAP

Augsburg

GERMANY

Munich

Salzburg

BENEDIKTENWAND

KARWENDEL ALPS

AUSTRIA

N

Innsbruck

Hall

TUXER ALPS

ZILLERTAL ALPS

Pfunders

0   20   40
km

Brenner
pass

Cortina

DOLOMITES

Bolzano

Alleghe

ITALY

SLOVENIA

Belluno

Trento

Pordenone

Gorizia

Treviso

Trieste

Verona

Venice

Mantua

Rovigo

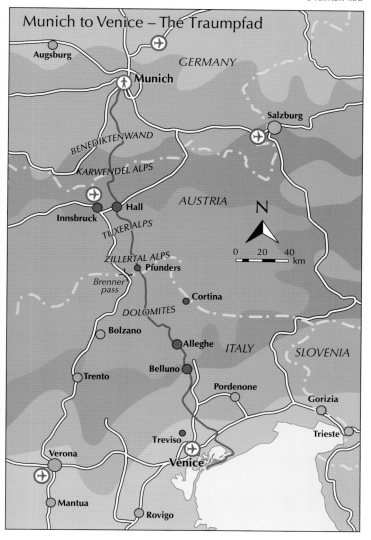

9

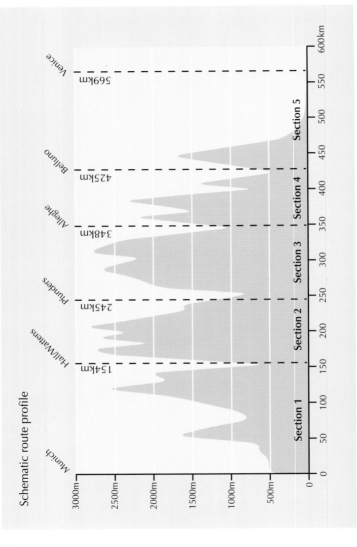

Schematic route profile

ROUTE SUMMARY TABLE

Stage		Distance (km)	Time	Ascent/Descent (m)	Page
Section 1 – Munich to the Inn Valley					
Stage 1	Munich to Wolfratshausen	34	8hr 10min	140/90	43
Stage 2	Wolfratshausen to Bad Tölz	28	7hr 10min	240/170	50
Stage 3	Bad Tölz to Tutzinger Hütte	21	7hr 40min	1250/570	55
Stage 4	Tutzinger Hütte to Vorderriß	18	7hr 20min	710/1270	62
Stage 5	Vorderriß to Karwendelhaus	24	7hr 10min	1050/50	67
Stage 6	Karwendelhaus to Hallerangerhaus	15	9hr	1550/1560	73
Stage 7A	Hallerangerhaus to Hall	14	4hr 30min	240/1450	81
Stage 7B	Hallerangerhaus to Wattens	19	6hr 10min	140/1460	84
Section totals		**154 (or 159)**	**7 days**	**5320/6620**	
Section 2 – Inn Valley to Pfunders					
Stage 8A	Hall to Glungezer Hütte	22	8hr 50min	2400/450	93
Stage 8B	Wattens to Lizumer Hütte	17	7hr 40min	1760/210	99
Stage 9	Glungezer Hütte to Lizumer Hütte	15	8hr 40min	750/1330	105
Stage 10	Lizumer Hütte to Tuxer Joch Haus	10	6hr 30min	1140/870	110
Stage 11A	Tuxer Joch Haus to the Olpererhütte	11	6hr 30min	1100/500	116

11

Stage		Distance (km)	Time	Ascent/Descent (m)	Page
Stage 11B	Tuxer Joch Haus to the Geraerhütte	10	4hr 40min	800/700	121
Stage 12A	Olpererhütte to Stein	13	5hr 30min	400/1310	124
Stage 12B	Geraerhütte to Stein	14	8hr 10min	1210/1960	128
Stage 13	Stein to Pfunders	20	8hr 10min	1200/1550	132
Section totals		**91 (or 71)**	**6 (or 5) days**	**10760/8880**	
Section 3 – Pfunders to Alleghe					
Stage 14	Pfunders to Kreuzwiesen Alm	24	8hr	1500/800	141
Stage 15	Kreuzwiesen Alm to Schlüterhütte	22	8hr 30min	1370/990	146
Stage 16	Schlüterhütte to Puezhütte	11	5hr	740/560	152
Stage 17	Puezhütte to Rifugio Boè	14	6hr 50min	1270/860	158
Stage 18	Rifugio Boè to Rifugio Viel dal Pan	9	4hr	400/840	164
Stage 19	Rifugio Viel dal Pan to Alleghe	24	5hr 50min	230/1670	168
Section totals		**103**	**6 days**	**5510/5720**	
Section 4 – Alleghe to Belluno					
Stage 20	Alleghe to Rifugio Tissi	13	6hr 10min	1780/350	179
Stage 21	Rifugio Tissi to Rifugio Bruto Carestiato	16	6hr	740/1160	184
Stage 22	Rifugio Bruto Carestiato to Rifugio Pian de Fontana	20	8hr	1200/1300	188

Stage	Distance (km)	Time	Ascent/Descent (m)	Page
Stage 23A	Rifugio Pian de Fontana to Rifugio 7th Alpini	14	8hr	2200/2100	195
Stage 23B	Rifugio Pian de Fontana to Belluno	10	4hr 40min	120/1650	199
Stage 24	Rifugio 7th Alpini to Belluno	14	4hr 20min	280/1250	230
Section totals	**77 (or 59)**	**5 (or 4) days**	**6320/7810**	

Section 5 – Belluno to Venice

Stage 25	Belluno to Rifugio Col Visentin	17	5hr 30min	1600/270	211
Stage 26	Rifugio Col Visentin to Tarzo	18	5hr 40min	130/1670	216
Stage 27	Tarzo to Ponte della Priulà	29	6hr 20min	550/750	221
Stage 28	Ponte della Priulà to Bocca Callalta	26	6hr 10min	40/110	228
Stage 29	Bocca Callalta to Jesolo	31	8hr	60/70	233
Stage 30	Jesolo to Venice	23	6hr	negligible	240
Section totals	**144**	**6 days**	**2380/2870**	
Overall total	**569**	**30 days**		

The colourful canals of Venice at journey's end (Stage 30)

INTRODUCTION

A view of Hintertux glacier from the Tux Alps (Stage 10)

Ever since Hannibal crossed the Alps the challenge of traversing Europe's biggest mountain range has attracted walkers from across the planet. Despite this, the Munich to Venice backpacking route – one of the most popular trans-alpine routes – is little known outside the German-speaking world. In Germany walkers regard it as the hiking experience of a lifetime. Each year hundreds of walkers of all shapes and sizes leave Munich's Mariënplatz, to arrive one month later in the Piazza San Marco in Venice. The walk is known as Der Traumpfad – the Dream Way – and its attractions

are immediately apparent. It links two of Europe's most iconic destinations with a journey across some of the best scenery in the Alps. From the heart of Bavaria, from beirgartens, wurst, and lederhosen, to the Adriatic and pro-secco, fritto misto and tiramisù – it's a journey across cultures as well as mountains.

Most long-distance treks involve compromise when it comes to scenery: breathtaking scenery doesn't usually organise itself along straight lines, particularly when the lines are 570km long. Accordingly, some of the days on the Traumpfad are less

Approaching the Schlüterhütte – the first hut in the Dolomites (Stage 15)

than perfect, particularly the last four on the approach to Venice, but most compare with the best in the Alps. The scenic fireworks start to go off on Stages 3 and 4 with the climb up into Benediktenwand 'pre-alps' with its amazing ridge walk, and again on Stages 5, 6 and 7 on the journey through the Karwendel and the climb up its highest mountain, the Birkkarspitz.

Without time to draw breath Stages 8 to 12 cross the Alpine spine itself with an amazing journey through the Tux and Zillertal Alps. In Italy now, and yet more rockets explode. The route traverses the Dolomites, arguably the most beautiful mountains in the world. Stages 14 to 23 are spent crossing the Puez and the Sella

groups, walking alongside the famous north face of the Marmolada, and finish with the Civetta (including its enormous west wall) and the Schiara group.

The Traumpfad is like a modern-day pilgrimage – a long walk to an iconic destination but without the religious overtones. Like Chaucer's pilgrims, walkers travel on a fairly standard schedule and so bump into each other night after night and exchange gossip and stories of their adventures. The company of other walkers, inspired by a common objective, is almost unavoidable and, for most participants, an attractive feature of the Munich to Venice route.

To top it all, the infrastructure is second to none. The Alps are where high-altitude trekking as a mass-participation sport was invented and walkers in their thousands have enjoyed 'Europe's playground' for well over a hundred years. Whether it's the paths, the waymarking, the steps and fixed steel ropes, or the alpine huts, there is nothing quite like it anywhere else – enabling ordinary walkers to go to extraordinary places.

HISTORY OF THE REGION

The walk from Munich to Venice passes through three countries – Germany, Austria and Italy – all of which went through intense changes from the mid-19th century which have a direct bearing on the character of the walk.

Munich, capital of Bavaria, is surprisingly 'imperial'. Bavaria was a distinct country until 1871 when a secret bribe from Bismark persuaded the high living and indebted Ludwig II (called the 'fairy tale king' because he built so many castles) to nominate Kaiser Wilhelm I as Emperor of a united Germany. Bavaria retains a special status in Germany to this day and its inhabitants will describe themselves as Bavarian first and German second.

The style of food and accommodation don't really change when you cross the border from Bavarian Germany into Austria and the two countries share much in terms of culture. Their recent history is also intertwined. The Austro-Hungarian Empire dominated the loose confederation of states that existed before the unification of Germany and, although the triumph of Bismark and Prussia, reversed the power hierarchy, the fate of the new Germany and the old Empire remained connected until after the First World War.

World War I dramatically reset the national boundaries crossed by the Traumpfad. Much more of the walk is now spent in Italy than it might have been! The total collapse of the vast Austro-Hungarian empire resulted in the border moving north with Italy absorbing German-speaking South Tyrol. This results today in an intensely confusing nomenclature from Stage 12 with mountain huts, mountains, towns, cities and food known by two (Italian and German) and sometimes three (Ladin, another local language) names.

The War settled the boundaries of modern Italy and also completed the process of Italian unification that had taken place over the previous 60 years. Italian historians also see it as the great nationalist war and the last part of the Traumpfad visits some key battle sites. Particularly important are the Marmolada – which was the scene of prolonged fighting on top of and underneath the glacier – and the River Piave, witness to the last great battle of the war, the Battle of Vittorio Veneto. The last three days of the route follow the Piave on the approach to Venice and the references to the triumph of Italian arms are impossible to miss.

The arrival of alpinism

Parallel to, and intertwined with the national histories of Germany, Austria and Italy is the history of alpinism, walking and the Alpine Clubs.

The attraction of the Alps to mountaineers can be traced back to the late 18th century and is described in a wonderful book *The Playground of Europe* by Sir Leslie Stephen. As well as being father to Virginia Woolf and Vanessa Bell, Stephen was one of the godfathers of British alpinism and his book, along with Edward Whymper's *Scrambles Amongst the Alps* is one of the classics of the genre. As well as describing great adventures it puts the 'discovery' of the Alps in the context of a wider search for a simpler but more heroic lifestyle that was going on throughout Europe, known as 'Romanticism'.

Stephen, Whymper and the British led the 'golden age' of climbing in the Alps, the time when, in the 1850s and 1860s, hundreds of peaks where 'conquered' for the first time. In Britain climbing and hiking was an elite activity but not so in Germany where the Romantic ideal of the mountains captured the imagination of the new middle class. The British Alpine Club was modelled on an English gentleman's club with a small select membership but the German equivalent grew rapidly into the world's largest mass membership sporting organisation. The new membership wanted access to the mountains and the huge infrastructure of mountain huts used today was largely built in the 30 years before the First World War (the names often reflect the local clubs that paid for them – such as the Berliner Hütte).

The German Alpine Club recruited members from the wider German-speaking world (including Austria), and hiking and climbing in the Alps was seen as a 'German' activity and closely associated with German nationalism. By the late 19th century this nationalism shamefully became associated with anti-semitism and a number of city and regional associations adopted an 'Aryan Paragraph' excluding non-Christian members.

The German Alpine Club, liked most civilian bodies, rallied round the flag at the outbreak of the World War I but the importance of the alpine front against Italy from 1915 gave alpinists a particular significance. Although a small proportion of the huge membership engaged in the fighting the involvement of Alpine Club members became the stuff of legend, reported and repeated through the club journals.

The collapse of the Austro-Hungarian Empire and the defeat of Germany was a particular blow to the heroes of the alpine front and one that many refused to accept. By the early 1920s the Alpine Club had become a battleground as the emerging Nazi party fought more moderate and left-leaning alpinists for its control. By 1924 Jews were effectively excluded from the Club and its huts.

By the 1930s, the German Alpine Club, like most sporting associations, had been absorbed into the Nazi totalitarian state. Alpinism, however, had a particular cultural status and mountaineers, willing to risk all for their sport and country, were seen as models for the new state. As a result, after the war Deutscher Alpenverein (the name dates back to 1938) was deemed a Nazi organisation by the Allies in 1945 and dissolved.

In the early 1950s, separate German (Deutscher Alpenverein) and Austrian (Oesterreichischer Alpenverien) Alpine Clubs were allowed to re-establish and together they continue to maintain and develop the incredible walking infrastructure of Austrian Alps. This includes not only the huts but also the footpaths, fixed ropes and waymarks. We wouldn't be able to walk from Munich to Venice without them.

THE INVENTION OF A MOUNTAIN PILGRIMAGE

The Traumpfad was the idea of a German man, Ludwig Grassler, who, after several false starts, walked it for first time 1974. His guide was first published 1977. An Alpinist himself, he was careful to construct a route that was both direct and spectacular. He succeeded and, like Wainwright's famous 'coast-to-coast' (across northern England), one man's vision has captured many thousands of imaginations.

Most of Ludwig's journey follows existing routes, some of which (like the Alta Via 1 and 2 across the Dolomites) are famous in their own right. Although there is no designated 'Munich to Venice' footpath – no specific set of waymarks signposting the route – it is easy to follow and, because it's more popular than many designated walks, it is well supported by locals. The route continues to evolve with slight differences in the different guidebooks and changes to reflect new circumstances. When accommodation closes, or a landslip destroys a section of the route, or a new footpath is opened, then the route responds.

THE ROUTE

There is more to the Traumpfad than a north–south traverse of the Alps but the mountains cannot help but dominate the experience.

It takes only two and a half days' walk alongside the River Isar to get from Munich to the mountains. You are then in the mountains for at least 20 consecutive days (depending on the choices you make about how to stage your journey). When you emerge, you follow the River Piave, over five days of flat walking, to get to Venice.

The Alps are a young and dynamic mountain range sitting right in the middle of Europe. They are the product of Africa's land mass thrusting northwards. A huge, multi-layered

Geisler Púez and the Forcella Roa (Stage 16)

ripple in Europe's tectonic plate has been driven skywards where, high and exposed, the elements wreak havoc and erosion is rapid, violent and fierce. The youngest, softest layers suffer the most and vast quantities of debris are transported out of the Alps by rivers and glaciers only to be returned as Africa continues to move north. The remnants of these younger layers, carved into mountains, are found on the northern and southern sides of the Alps with the toughest oldest rock revealed in the exposed core in the middle.

Despite looking quite different to one another the mighty Karwendel on the northern side of the core and the Dolomites to the south are closely related. Both are of similar age, formed in similar circumstances, and both are composed of types of limestone. The lagoons where the Dolomites were formed, however, produced a higher proportion of magnesium and that gave these mountains their distinct shape and colour.

The limestone on top of the core of the Alps, running east–west, has long been stripped away and older layers exposed. This is what you see when you cross the Tux and Zillertal Alps, where instead of limestone the mountains consist of much older metamorphic gneiss, slate and granite.

Although the age of the rocks on view is measured in tens of millions of years the process that turned them into mountains is more recent. This is a landscape where for most of the year the predominant colour is white, and which only a few thousand years ago was almost totally covered by an ice cap. Glaciers still cut their way into mountainsides today. Even with global warming the process that formed today's mountains (only the highest of which would have protruded through the ice cap) is still going on.

Identifying the various mountains is one of the challenges and joys of the Traumpfad. Some of mountains 'visited' have an iconic status that renders them instantly recognisable (such as Marmolada, the highest mountain in the Dolomites, or Pelmo, the most beautiful), but others are important in the wider pantheon of Alpine peaks (for example Bikkarspitz, the highest mountain in the Karwendel, the Hochfeiler, the biggest in the Zillertal, and Civetta the famous west wall of which is the highest of the last mountain stage of the route). Tentatively naming a mountain approached from the north, confirming its designation as it gets closer and saying goodbye to it from the south is a process that can extend over many days.

THE ALPINE SEASONS

The position of the Alps in the middle of Europe has a profound effect on both the seasons and the weather, not just in the mountains themselves but also in the surrounding regions.

Winter lasts a long time but the transition to a short summer (and walking season) is fast and furious. The gap between the treeline (1800m) and the snowline (2800m), where

Pelmo – the most beautiful mountain in the Dolomites? (Stage 22)

happily the route spends much of its time, becomes a riot of colour as alpine flowers and shrubs react to the warmth and sunshine and burst into bloom. Although no longer as important to the local economy as winter skiing, these summer alpine meadows still sustain the *transhumance* as beautiful brown cattle (the Swiss breed Simmental) are bought up from the valleys in July for ten weeks of summer grazing before returning in September just before the first snow.

The snow and the consequent surge of meltwater have an enormous impact on Traumpfad. Starting in Munich the route follows the River Isar whose fast-flowing grey water, destined for the Danube and the Black Sea, betrays its origins in the Karwendel limestone. The route then crosses the Inn, the most important tributary of the Danube, snakes above the huge reservoir, the Schlegeisspeicher, fed by the glacier on the north side of the Hochfeiler, before crossing the watershed on the border with Italy. From here the water heads south and then east to the Adriatic and the Mediterranean. The walk finishes, as it started, with a riverside walk, but this time along an Italian river, the Piave.

The Alps occupy a battleground between weather systems: the Atlantic, Continental and Mediterranean. In the summer you can expect (but not rely on) good weather. As a general rule it's wetter in the north near Germany and drier in Italy, but extremes of weather,

Classic view of the River Isar from the Rißsattel (Stage 4)

including snow, need to be anticipated. As the temperature increases
in July and August, thunderstorms are
not uncommon and September is the
most settled month.

ALPINE FLOWERS, ANIMALS AND BIRDS

The epic film *The Sound of Music*
may be associated with Salzburg but
iconic scenes in flower-filled Alpine
meadows can also be enjoyed on the
Traumpfad.

The edelweiss (symbol of the
German Alpine Club), with its creamy

felty petals in a star formation, may
be the most famous flower but it's
only one of over 1500 varieties that
all share an uncanny ability to survive
extremely low temperatures. Easier to
spot than edelweiss are blue trumpet
gentians or harebells. Perhaps a little
gaudy and much larger is the alpine
orange lily. You may also see, growing heroically on inhospitable scree,
the golden yellow Rhaetian poppy,
larger flowered yellow ox-eye or the
globeflower. Attractive even to those
with the most casual interest in flowers are orchids, the most spectacular
of which is probably the lady's slipper

*A selection of Alpine flowers: Bavarian gentian; Apiaceae; white campion;
alpine scabious; gentian; fragrant orchid; yellow alpine poppy; edelweiss;
ground cistus; woolly thistle; silver thistle (Photos: Max and Frances Harre)*

Sunbathing marmots

orchid with its maroon and yellow petals. At the treeline, conifers dominate: silver fir, arolla pine and larch are the main species with dwarf pine higher up on the scree.

Like the flowers, animals have to be capable of surviving extreme conditions living on slim pickings. Perhaps the most prolific, and certainly the easiest to spot, are marmots. They look like a tubby meerkat (with a similar upright posture) but in fact are a type of squirrel. They live in colonies and whistle to each other as a warning. The colony leader, standing upright, spots or smells danger, issues a whistle that often echoes around a rock face, and the colony of marmots promptly disappears underground. You will certainly see and hear them along the route.

Less common and generally seen only in the distance are the chamois and ibex. Both in the past have been hunted to near extinction and both are happily in recovery. They are part of the goat-antelope family and share with their domestic brethren a distinct goat-like smell. As well as being incredibly nimble over rocks and up the side of mountains (occasionally unhelpfully dislodging stones) they graze in places where even in summer there is little in the way of grass. The male ibex has much bigger horns than chamois and the chamois has a distinctive black strip on its face.

Also specially adapted for alpine conditions and quite common is the black alpine salamander and its more spectacular cousin the fire salamander (black with gold patches).

The alpine salamander is the only European amphibian to give birth to live young (usually two of them) emerging after developing inside the mother for three years – a longer gestation period even than the elephant (just over two years).

The Alps are not a particularly rich habitat for birds. Most common is the alpine chough, a small hyperactive crow specifically adapted for high altitude,. Also important is the nutcracker, a bird that looks similar to a starling, which plays a key role in the life of the arolla pine distributing, in a good year, up to 100,000 seeds in holes up to a metre under the snow at the perfect depth for germination. The nutcracker has a brilliant memory. It returns for most of the seeds but leaves enough to secure future generations of the tree. If you see a raptor it is likely to be a common buzzard although there are also honey buzzards around. There are about 350 pairs of golden eagle in the Austrian Alps so if you're lucky you might see one of them as well.

WHAT'S THE WALKING LIKE?

As well as passing through superlative scenery the Munich to Venice trail neatly combines challenge with accessibility. Although it stays within the magic zone between treeline (1800m) and snowline (2800m) for much of the way, valleys do have to be crossed and descents made, with varying levels of ease. It's a safe and accessible route,

Climbing out the Val de Tita (Stage 17) with the help of fixed cables

providing sensible caution is taken
with the weather, and largely avoids
the skiing areas which scar the landscape in many places (the chief excep-
tions being the Sella massif and the
Hintertux Glacier). Although the route
is rarely crowded, this is not a walk for
those seeking solitude, despite spend-
ing so many days above 2000m.

HOW HARD IS IT?

Ludwig designed his Munich to
Venice backpacking route for 'any
able-bodied walker'. By this he
meant walkers who were happy to
walk for around thirty days, carrying
seven kilogrammes for around seven
hours a day and climbing an average
of a thousand metres a day. Ludwig
was a German and an Alpinist so he
assumed walkers would have a head
for heights, which is an essential
requirement on several short exposed
stretches. On the most exposed sections there are fixed steel ropes and
pegs driven into a rock face to help
you progress. This is a common feature of Alpine walking and something
the average German or Austrian takes
for granted but which you might find
challenging the first time you come
across it. Most of these stretches are
near the most spectacular sections of
the route, however, and it would be a
shame to miss them.

While a reasonable level of
fitness, a head for heights and a
desire for adventure are all essential requirements for anyone tackling

the Traumpfad, it does make a good
choice for walkers planning their
first independent trek in the Alps.
Experience of mountain walking is
an advantage but it is not necessary
and this guide makes no assumptions
about previous experience.

HOW LONG WILL IT TAKE?

The Traumpfad is 569km long and
involves 27,000 metres of ascent. The
most popular German schedule takes
29 days but assumes that walkers take
the chairlift on one section of the walk
(Stage 7). The schedule in this guide is
similar but assumes that some walkers
at least will want to walk 'every step
of the way' from Munich to Venice
and an extra day has therefore been
included.

Stages are designed to start and
finish where accommodation is
available. The daily walking times
are between 5hrs 30mins and 9hrs.
Matching these times will be harder
at the beginning of the walk than
at the end, and options for merg-
ing days start to increase as the walk
progresses.

A key consideration will be your
attitude to chairlifts and the closely
linked question of 'purity' when it
comes to walking every step of the
way. There are at least four big climbs
that could be replaced by a chairlift
and the time saved could either be
spent with a beer in a mountain hut
enjoying the views or walking further
along the path and saving a day – the

Descent from Schlauchkarsattel (Stage 16)

question is whether you will still be able to claim that you walked from Munich to Venice!

Superstrong, superfast walkers will beat the times in the schedule but that doesn't help if there isn't accommodation further along the route. If you are desperate to complete the trip in one go but don't have the 31 to 33 days needed (30 days with some contingency and allowance for travel at either end), the schedule can be reduced by about 4 to 5 days without needing to carry a tent. The tool for doing this is the Route Planner in Appendix A.

Alternatively, if you would prefer to tackle the route in chunks (described as Sections in this guide), there are five natural divisions, each defined by good entry and exit points for public transport. These are:

Munich to Hall	7 days
Hall to Vandoies (Niedervintl)	6 days
Niedervintl to Alleghe	6 days
Alleghe to Belluno	5 days
Belluno to Venice	6 days

WHEN TO GO

The likelihood of snow on the passes determines the short length of the Alpine walking season – from early July through to the third week in September. The huge network of Alpine huts only opens when the passes clear of snow and the walkers start to turn up.

Although it can vary significantly from year to year there is greater likelihood of lingering snow in July. Alpine thunderstorms are more frequent in

Summer snow on the Geierjoch

July and August, and September is the most settled month. The peak season, coinciding with holidays, is August, so timing a trip to make the best use of September (the quietest month) makes sense. This would involve starting in Munich towards the end of August and finishing the alpine traverse by the third week in September. The only downside is that the alpine flowers will be past their best.

ACCOMMODATION

Most nights on the schedule described in this guide, and especially those spent at altitude, will involve staying in a mountain hut. If this is your first long-distance trip in the Alps, mountain huts may take some getting used to but the social aspect of sharing a 'mountain pilgrimage' with a varied group of, largely German, fellow travellers, in family groups, couples or walking alone, could be said to be a key part of the Munich to Venice experience.

By sharing rooms and evening meals everyone soon gets to know each other and a mutually supportive network is formed. Germans generally speak good English and will happily help explain the difference between Leberknödel and Speckknödel. Groups emerge and evolve as walkers on different schedules arrive and depart.

In addition to mountain huts, some nights will be spent in delightful small alpine hotels. These are comfortable and provide a welcome change from the huts. In the summer season they offer surprisingly good value. And if you prefer to avoid the communal living, alternative itineraries which minimise the use of huts are described in the introductions to some of the sections.

Charges

A reasonable rule of thumb is to budget 50 euros a day although this depends on what you choose to eat and drink rather than your choice of accommodation. There is little difference between the cost of a small hotel and a mountain hut, although sleeping in large and often noisier hut dormitories can be cheaper.

Many huts are owned by the German, Austrian or Italian Alpine clubs where Alpine Club members get a discount. Given the number of huts on the itinerary, this discount and other membership benefits (including insurance), it's worth joining an Alpine Club (see Appendix B). If

A convivial hut scene (Photo: Max and Frances Harre)

you're British the simplest option is to join the British section of the Austrian Alpine Club – the modest fee includes insurance.

Booking ahead

Booking into the mountain huts ahead is generally straightforward and fairly casual, particularly once you get to Italy. Currently some of the German and Austrian huts ask for a deposit via bank transfer, which can be expensive outside the Eurozone, and if you point this out they usually let you off. The plan is for a single booking system to be established which will take credit cards. This could be in place as soon as 2016. For the latest information and advice on booking huts go to the Alpine Club website (www.alpine-club.org.uk). If for whatever reason a booking can't be honoured then

simply ring and explain. It's never a surprise but you should let your hosts know.

HUT LIFE

Mountain huts date back to the explosion of Alpine tourism in the late 19th century and were mainly developed by the German/Austrian Alpenverein (Alpine Club). The nearest non-alpine equivalent is a youth hostel. There are hundreds of them scattered across the Alps and, typically built before the emergence of town planners, they often command a dramatic location. They provide food, beer, accommodation and usually a shower (in limestone areas water is sometimes in short supply). Sleeping accommodation is in open dormitories or smaller rooms although you should expect

A typically stunning hut location – the Olpererhütte (Stage 11)

to share even in the smaller rooms. Huts are a key part of the alpine tradition and come with a number of quirky rules. They are, however, very convivial, never run out of beer and after a good day in the mountains they provide an opportunity for some sleep (depending on your room-mates).

The first hut, the Tutzinger, provides a foretaste of what's to come. Once you've arrived and armed yourself with a beverage it's time to look at the menu and contemplate hut cuisine. It changes gradually after you cross into Italy but the Tyrolean influences persist for some time. It is not fine dining and is best described as 'hearty'. Standard fare includes: soups (Suppe) with large dumplings – either Leberknödel (liver dumpling) or Speckknödel (ham dumpling); Gulasch, often served with dumplings (Semmelknödel); spaghetti Bolognese and, of course, large sausages (Bratwurst) served with bread, mustard and sauerkraut. It's not ideal for vegetarians. In German and Austrian huts the Bergsteigeressen (literally 'mountain climber's food') is usually the lowest cost option on the menu. Consisting of some sort of meat served with pasta, dumplings or potatoes, it is filling and good value. On the German side of the border, the best part of the meal – a major Austrian/German contribution to world welfare – is the desert where the nightly choice between wonderful Apfelstrudel (apple pastry) or Kaiserschmarrn, (a shredded pancake favoured by Emperor Franz Joseph) is a regular challenge.

The main dormitory in the Tutzinger consists of two-storey

platforms each populated, cheek by jowl, with lines of mattresses. Unlike most UK youth hostels, dormitories are not single sex. Bedding is provided but guests are expected to bring their own sheet sleeping bags (Hütten Sac) – some people also bring their own sleeping bags although the rooms can be very warm. Like most huts there is a drying room and a boot room. Hut etiquette includes not wearing outdoor shoes indoors and walking poles are left in the boot room.

Lights are turned out at 10pm. It's not worth retiring earlier as the noise around bedtime can make sleep difficult. Getting to sleep may be a challenge – unfamiliar snoring will take a bit of getting used to – so it's best to pack earplugs.

Breakfast, served at 7.30am, is interesting if not particularly exciting. It involves tea or coffee, bread and jam, some sort of cereal and processed ham similar to the subject of a famous Monty Python sketch. Austrian bread, like Austrian cakes, is an art form but for some reason the higher art forms don't reach the higher altitudes and hut bread is of a particularly heavy and dark variety.

Kaiserschmarrn

PLANNING YOUR WALK

Perhaps the first thing to decide, particularly if walking alone or as a couple, is whether to have a schedule at all. Instead of planning every day in advance and booking the trip ahead it is possible simply to turn up and assume that there will be space available, or you ring ahead one or two days in advance. In this way you can capitalise on good weather and walk further. Not booking ahead, however, naturally carries the risk that you will not be able to stay where you want to. This could be a problem at some huts in the Dolomites on August weekends, especially if you are walking as part of a group. Also, if you wish to sleep in family rooms rather than dormitories booking ahead is recommended.

If you're planning to walk the route in one go, factors to consider when working out your schedule are:
• whether you are prepared to use any of the chairlifts or take a bus at any point;
• whether you prefer to avoid the mountain huts where alternatives can be found (particularly important in the Dolomites in August);
• whether you plan to walk any of the variants;
• how many hours a day you want to walk.

Another consideration is whether to schedule spare days, either as rest days or to accommodate potential bad weather. For example a schedule could include a provision for two or three nights at Alleghe, a pretty

Just some of the friends made along a first through-walk from Munich to Venice

lakeside town located in the middle of the Dolomites with plenty of accommodation. If bad weather then means sitting out a day's walking earlier in the trip one of the days at Alleghe can be dropped without throwing out the rest of your itinerary.

One thing to check before finalising a schedule is whether or not 'shooting days' are taking place in the Tux Alps. A military exercise range still exists there and very occasionally the troops are using live ammunition and access is prohibited. All the routes cross the range and it's worth checking at www. wattenberg.tirol.gv.at and following the link to 'Truppenübungsplatz Lizum Walchen'.

WHAT TO TAKE

The golden rule is only take what is needed. Weight is a key consideration and the greater the load, the bigger the strain on the body particularly the knees. Weigh everything and restrict the total load (excluding water) to no more than 7kg.

When packing prepare for wet and cold weather. On a 30-day trip across the Alps you will almost certainly get some wet weather at some point and in July and early August it can be thundery. It can also be cold and snow, particularly above 2000m, is not unusual. In addition to good quality waterproofs pack a fleece or a lightweight down jacket, a warm hat and gloves.

It addition to the cold and wet prepare for the sun and include a brimmed hat, high-factor sunscreen, lipsalve and sunglasses. With any luck the cold and wet weather gear will stay at the bottom of your rucksack and shorts and T-shirts will be the order of the day.

For emergencies carry a head torch (also useful in the huts), a whistle and a compact first aid kit.

For the huts, as well as personal toiletries, pack a lightweight towel, a sheet sleeping bag and earplugs. Outdoor shoes aren't allowed inside and although indoor shoes are provided some sort of lightweight shoe will be needed for the hotels and for walking around Venice.

At the beginning of each stage of route description there is a tip about where you can get refreshments during the day. There is usually somewhere to stop but you should always carry emergency rations and snacks. Everyone will have their own solution but a bar of chocolate hidden at the bottom of the rucksack (out of the sun and to avoid temptation) is mine.

A comfortable rucksack is an essential item but it's more likely to be comfortable if the total load is only 6 to 7kg. It needs a waterproof cover. Stuff sacks within the rucksack might also help; they hardly weigh anything and impose a bit of order when things are getting packed in the morning.

Footwear should also be light. Remember a kilogram on your feet is equivalent to four on your back. Heavy boots in particular should be avoided given the long hot days on

Climbing the Geirjoch in August (Stage 10)

33

the approach to Venice. Many walkers (me included) have abandoned boots altogether for summer walking, opting for 'approach shoes' or fell-running shoes instead. Lightweight footwear means feet stay cooler, skin is less likely to blister and you can walk further without getting tired.

FINDING YOUR WAY

For most of its journey the Traumpfad follows well-defined footpaths. The last section, from Belluno to Venice, involves some road walking but mostly on quiet roads with little traffic. There are occasional Munich–Venice (München–Venedig) signs but the route is not officially waymarked. It is, however, easy to follow and navigation should not be a problem.

Using GPS

Although most walkers now have a smartphone many still don't use the GPS functionality but GPS is the cheapest and most effective way of taking the stress out of navigation. If you already have an Android or Apple smartphone you can download a GPS app and buy the required digital maps.

A key consideration, in choosing an app, is the range of maps provided particularly when the route travels through several countries. A good choice, and one used when doing the research for this guide, is a product called Viewranger (www. viewranger.com). The Viewranger website includes a map store and has a growing portfolio of maps from around the world including Germany,

Approaching Dun (Stage 13)

The central Karwendel Ridge

Austria and Italy. The route is covered by maps of a comparable quality to the paper maps (most are the same but a digital version) until just before Alleghe. From Alleghe to Venice 'Open Maps' can be used (follow the instructions on the Viewranger site for loading these maps). They don't provide as much information as the paper maps but they are still useful.

In addition to a smartphone and a GPS app loaded with the right maps you need the route itself. This is available for free, stage by stage, on the Cicerone website at www.cicerone. co.uk/804/gpx.

If you haven't used the GPS facility don't leave it to the last minute before your trip to find out how it works. Smartphone GPS doesn't use 'data roaming' so you don't need to have that facility turned on. The battery on the smartphone should be adequate for a day's walking particularly if you remember to turn off any features that you're not using. (Phones permanently searching for a wi-fi connection are consuming a lot of energy.) If you are nervous about battery life then take a supplementary battery and recharge the smartphone as needed or, if walking with someone else with a smartphone, have a duplicate version of the GPS as backup.

Using printed maps

Some walkers will want the additional security of paper maps (despite the extra weight) and printed maps will provide more context for the journey. Acquiring a comprehensive set of maps for a route travelling through three countries is not, however, a straightforward task and there is no single publisher supplying maps for the whole route.

Section 1

Kompass Maps (www.shop.kompass.de):
180 Lake Starnberg – Ammersee and 182 Isarwinkel, Bad Tölz, Lenggries (1:50,000)
Freytag & Berndt (www.freytagberndt.com):
WK 322 Wetterstein – Karwendel – Seefeld – Leutasch – Garmisch Partenkirchen (1:50,000)

Section 2

Freytag & Berndt (www.freytagberndt.com):
WK 322 Wetterstein – Karwendel – Seefeld – Leutasch – Garmisch Partenkirchen (1:50,000)
WK 241 Innsbruck – Stubai – Sellrain – Brenner (1:50.000)
WK 152 Mayrhofen – Zillertaler Alpen – Gerlogs – Krimml – Zell im Zillertal (1:50,000)
Tabacco TK 037 Pfunderer Berge/Monti di Fundres, Hochfeiler/Gran Pilastro (1:25,000).

Section 3

Freytag & Berndt (www.freytagberndt.com):
Tabacco TK 030 Brixen/Bressanone, Villnössertal/Val di Funes (1:25.000)
WK S5 Grödner Tal (1:50,000)

Section 4

Freytag & Berndt (www.freytagberndt.com):
TK 015 Marmolada – Pelmo – Civetta – Moiazza (1:25,000)

TK 025 Dolomiti di Zoldo, Cadorine e Agordine (1:25,000)
TK 024 Prealpi e Dolomiti Bellunesi (1:25,000)

Section 5

Map Fox (www.mapfox.de)
Cartine Zanetti – 5 Vittorio Veneto (1:30,000)
Cartine Zanetti – 3 Conegliano (1:30,000).

If you need to ask the way, German is the language spoken locally in Bavaria, Austria and South Tyrol, with Italian becoming the dominant language on the approach to Alleghe. Signposts also include a third language, Ladin, in a small area to the south of the Italian border with Austria. Germans, Austrians and Italians all speak good English and indeed many Italians and Germans communicate with each other in English.

USING THIS GUIDE

The 569km of the journey from Munich to Venice has been described here in five sections each broken down into a stage which correlates to a day's walking. Sections begin with a brief introduction, overview map and summary information including your options for varying the itinerary. Each stage begins with an information box – giving basic data including distance, walking time and total ascent/descent – and a brief introduction to give you a feel for the day's walking. Each stage also has a difficulty grading:

Alpine lakes below the Alpeiner Scharte (Stage 12B)

- easy – essentially flat
- moderate – could involve physical exertion but with no exposed walking
- challenging – a head for heights required and could involve exposed sections.

There then follows a step-by-step description of the route including information about the facilities available along the route.

The route descriptions should be read in conjunction with the route maps which are reproduced at 1:100,000 scale, with a handful of maps at 1:50,000 for greater clarity. These show all the features highlighted in bold in the route descriptions, as well as using occasional numbered points for reference where a navigation decision is required at a

place without an obvious feature. The maps and route descriptions, used in conjunction with printed maps or GPS information, should help you make sense of what you see on the ground.

Also included are profiles of each stage of the route that show the climbs involved and the time taken to get from one key point to the next. Once in the mountains it should be easy to see how your performance compares with the timings given and adapt the guide timings to your own pace.

The route summary table at the start of the book gives a quick overview of the distance, walking time and ascent/descent for each stage and section. Various appendices are also provided to help you get the most out of your Munich to Venice experience. Appendix A – the trek planner

Panorama Hohenweg (Stage 12A)

– provides a schedule of stages along with points with accommodation along the route, giving distances and estimated walking times between them. This is designed to help you plan alternative itineraries. On some parts of the route the limited amount of accommodation means that the German schedule described in the 30 stages in this guide has to be followed but on other parts you have a real choice. Appendix B brings together the contact details of the facilities referred to in the route descriptions and the trek planner and Appendix C is a list of other useful contacts to help you plan your perfect Munich to Venice mountain pilgrimage.

1 MUNICH TO THE INN VALLEY

Descending to Peteralm (Stage 4)

First sight of the Alps (Stage 2)

This first section of the route is an ideal way to start a major multi-day hike. The first two days are uncomplicated and give you a chance to warm up for the alpine adventure ahead.

The walk starts in Munich, Germany's third biggest city, dynamic, fast growing and very accessible. Most walkers travelling from abroad will probably arrive a day early in time for an early start next day and, if so, there is plenty to see. Consider looking at St Johann Nepomuk, better known as the Asam Church, a beautiful and very sumptuous Baroque church or, if you want to limber up, take a walk through the English Garden, one of the largest urban parks in the world.

Section 1 could be broken down into three distinct legs. The first takes two and half days and follows the River Isar south from Munich to Lenggries. Despite starting in the middle of Munich the route is surprisingly quiet and for the most part follows a pretty riverside walk. It travels through the Isar Tal Verein a 'citizens' park' acquired through money raised by subscription in 1902. A response to concerns that the environment was being damaged by industrial development, it was one of the first parks of its kind in the world. The walk is a long one so expect hot feet and blisters if you're not careful.

The second leg crosses the Benediktenwand, part of the Bavarian pre-Alps. The term 'pre-Alps' suggests 'foothills' but these are proper mountains. After two and half days of flat walking an 800m climb will come as a shock, a shock compounded by arguably the most demanding ridge walk of the whole Traumpfad.

The third leg leaves Germany and heads into Austria, crossing the Karwendel and tackling another exciting climb up to the Birkkarspitz.

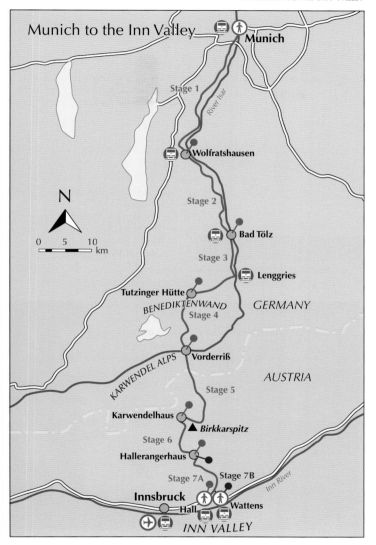

Munich to the Inn Valley

Munich

Stage 1

River Isar

Wolfratshausen

N

0   5   10
km

Stage 2

Bad Tölz

Stage 3

Lenggries

Tutzinger Hütte

BENEDIKTENWAND   GERMANY

Stage 4

Vorderriß

KARWENDEL ALPS   AUSTRIA

Stage 5

Karwendelhaus

▲ *Birkkarspitz*

Stage 6

Hallerangerhaus

Stage 7A   Stage 7B

Innsbruck   Inn River

Hall   Wattens

INN VALLEY

A long and stunning descent down the valley to Kastenalm follows before climbing next day over the Lafatscherjoch and into the Inn Valley.

ACCESS AND ACCOMMODATION

If you want to walk this first section in isolation, getting to and from the Inn Valley, a main transit route through Austria, is easy. Options include (from either Hall or Wattens) a train to Innsbruck airport or a train to Munich for a return flight.

Accommodation is in a mix of mountain huts and small alpine hotels. The Karwendel Haus, just before the Birkkarspitz, is particularly good, and you can get a two-person room if you book early enough.

Taking the easy way up

42

STAGE 1

Munich to Wolfratshausen

Start	Marienplatz (521m)
Distance	34km
Ascent/Descent	140m/90m
Difficulty	Easy
Walking time	8hr 10min
Maximum altitude	574m
Refreshments	There are plenty of places along the route to stop for lunch but if you'd prefer a picnic then Pullach has a particularly good baker and tempting local cheesecake.
Routefinding	The route is flat and easy to follow and there are several types of waymark providing direction to Wolfratshausen. Beware, however, no single set of waymarks leads to your destination and a wrong turn, annoying on what is a long day, is possible. The most helpful signs are the yellow Isartal Verein markers. Also useful are the Jacobswege signs (part of the trans-European St James' Way network).

Despite the fact that Stage 1 starts right in the heart of the third largest city in Germany this first stage is an enjoyable one. Making use of a long green finger that follows the River Isar through the city, it doesn't feel urban and makes a pleasant way to warm up for the journey ahead.

The walk starts at the **Marienplatz** (521m), Munich's main city centre square.

The square is dominated by the 'new' **City Hall**, a huge neo-Gothic building constructed towards the end of the 19th century. In the summer the square is generally packed with tourists, so taking unobstructed farewell pictures can be a challenge.

Leave the square on its southeast side and head along the Tal past Macdonalds, Burger King and the

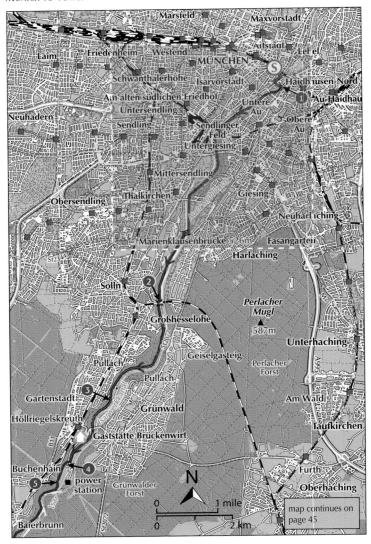

map continues on
page 45

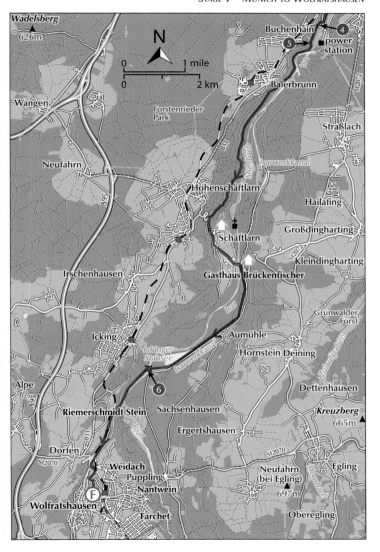

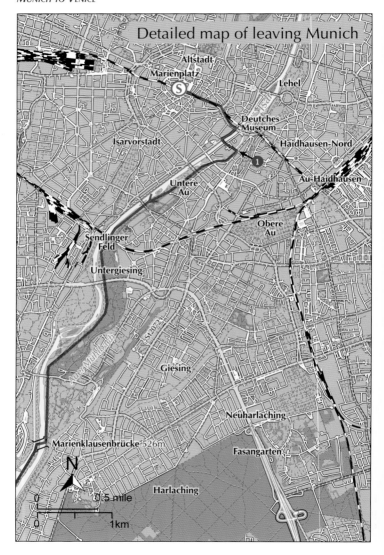

Detailed map of leaving Munich

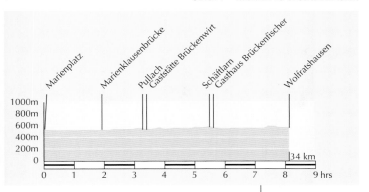

Schneiderweiss Brauhaus, one of the city's best known drinking establishments. Pass the old city gates (Isartor) and after crossing a potentially busy junction continue south-east down the Isartorplatz into the Zweibrückenstraße and to the bridge over the **River Isar**. Don't cross the bridge but turn right, heading down the Erhardstraße. After 300m turn left over a bridge and pass through the courtyard of the **Deutsches Museum** and then over another bridge (the museum is on an island in the river). Turn right after the bridge (**1**) onto a footpath running parallel with a cycle path and head southwest. Although you are still in the city your hard surface walking has now finished.

Continue southwest along a riverside walkway for 4km. Don't stray onto the cycle track which can be busy with cyclists rushing into the city. These cyclists take no prisoners. ▸

After passing underneath five bridges the route reaches a wooden footbridge, the **Marienklausenbrücke**, and crosses to the other side. The bridge is a local version of the more famous Pont des Art in Paris where devoted lovers leave engraved padlocks.

Follow a gravel path running south southwest between the river and the Isar canal. After 2km the route passes under a railway bridge and, at the same time, crosses a bridge over the canal (**2**) continuing south on its right hand side.

A sign of Renate and Fredi's love on the Marienklausenbrücke

The massive church on the opposite side of the river is the late 19th-century neo-Romanesque Maximilian Kirche.

47

After 2km (**3**) a sign points right to a path that heads up a bank and into the centre of **Pullach** where food can be found if needed. Follow the canal path for another kilometre to the **Gaststätte Brückenwirt** (reached after passing under a road bridge).

Continue south for 1.5km along the side of the canal until the path reaches a road (**4**). Turn right and follow the road for a short distance up a hill. Cross to the other side of the road to join a path that climbs up and around a very elegant hydroelectric power station. At a junction at the crest of the hill (**5**) take the left fork and follow a gently descending forest road through trees back down to what is now the river rather than the canal.

The forest road you've been following now turns into a narrow forest path (with limited waymarking) that can be muddy in places. Continue south to join another forest road and climb gently along it to a metalled one. Turn left onto the road and follow it down into the village of **Schäftlarn**.

The large and impressive building in the middle of the village was a **Benedictine Monastery** founded in 701 and is now a school.

The Klosterbräu Stüberl (**www.klosterbraeus tueberl-schaeftlarn.de**, tel 49 8178 3694) is a traditional Bavarian gasthof specialising in the local cuisine (in particular duck and carp dishes). It also provides accommodation.

Continue through the village alongside the road and southeast back to the river. Before crossing the bridge have a look at the installation in the car park and display boards on the River Isar.

On the other side of the bridge is the Gasthaus Brückenfischer (**www.bruckenfischer.de**, tel 49 8178 3635) another traditional Bavarian gasthof providing both food and accommodation.

Turn right after the bridge and pass through the car park in front of the gasthof. Follow a path that runs between the wild river and the banks of the elevated canal (a path also runs along the bank of the canal). Various boards describe different aspects of the river's natural history but the best is the last where a series of boxes with buttons emit bird songs. This installation marks the point where the route climbs to the top of the canal bank and joins a path heading south to the Ickinger Weir (**6**), reached after 2km.

Choose your birdsong along the River Isar

The weir has to be crossed. To do this you have to go through a metal door which opens onto concrete stairs and a footbridge through a wooden superstructure that covers the workings of the weir. It's an unlikely route but a sign to Wolfratshausen on the other side provides the reassurance that it's the right one.

Continue for 3km into **Wolfratshausen** passing the beauty spot at **Riemerschmidt Stein** after a kilometre.

WOLFRATSHAUSEN 574M

Wolfratshausen sits at the confluence of the Isar and Loisach rivers and has been a significant market town since the 13th century.

It has all the key services including a railway station. Most German walkers stay at the Gasthof Humpbräu (**www.humplbraeu.de**, tel 49 8171 483290) near the church on the west bank of the Isar. Apparently Ludwig Grassler, designer of the original Munich to Venice route in 1974, now lives in Wolfratshausen and can sometimes be found there welcoming walkers. Also good, and very comfortable, is the Hotel Isartaler Hof (breakfast only, **www.hotel-isartaler-hof.de**, tel 49 8171 23 88 122) located to the east of the train station.

STAGE 2
Wolfratshausen to Bad Tölz

Start	Wolfratshausen railway station (574m)
Distance	28km
Ascent/Descent	240m/170m
Difficulty	Easy
Walking time	7hr 10min
Maximum altitude	574m
Refreshments	There is nowhere to stop along the way today so plan for a picnic lunch. There are plenty of places to buy provisions in Wolfratshausen.
Routefinding	The ITV waymarks provide useful reminders that the right route is being followed although again you need to watch out for cycle route signs that at times, would take you in the wrong direction.

Another day and another walk along the River Isar. The highlight is a particularly beautiful stretch, halfway along, where the route climbs above the river and looks down on it through ancient beech and pine.

From the train station head south over Sauerlecher Strasse and follow a path along the side of the railway line south

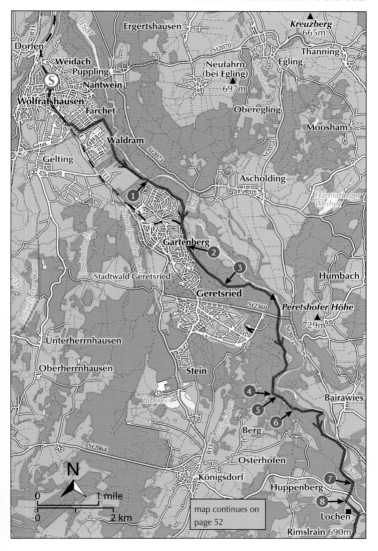

map continues on
page 52

51

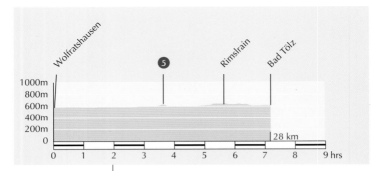

and then southeast for 1.3km. Turn left into Heidestraße and immediately right into Margeritenstraße. Continue southeast for 700m to a footbridge over the **Loisach-Isar Canal**. Don't cross it but turn left and head east along its northern bank.

After 800m walking alongside the canal cross a footbridge and follow a footpath southeast along the western

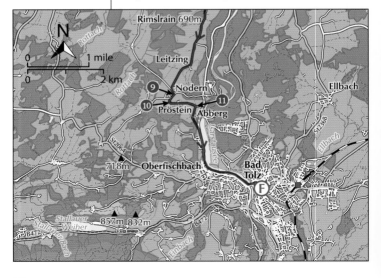

Steep descent through beech trees

bank of the River Isar for 2.4km towards **Gartenberg**. When the footpath finishes continue along the Straße Isardamm for about 100m (**1**), join a path on the left hand side and follow it through trees down to the river. This path then rejoins Straße Isardamm and follows it south for a kilometre. At an ITV waymark (easily missed) (**2**) turn left and follow a forest path (look out for some World War II bunkers in the woods along the way) southeast for a kilometre to where the path splits (**3**). Turn left here and head east along a smaller path through trees, now small and scrubby, down to the river again. ▸ Follow the path for 1.4km to a road and cross it.

At the river a short stretch of the original path had been washed away in 2014 but if it has not been reinstated it can be rejoined after a short detour through the trees.

From the road continue south for another 1.4km through trees (the path is cutting across a meander in the river) to where the path starts to climb through beech trees up a relatively steep path. After a 60m climb (**4**) (690m) turn left onto a forest road and follow it south for 200m before turning left onto a path (**5**). ▸

The views north from here are excellent and perfectly positioned benches make it a good place to stop for lunch.

From the benches follow the path steeply down the hillside, cross a bridge over a stream and head east across a meadow towards the river. Turn sharply left (**6**) from what looks like the main trail and follow a narrow path

53

With luck the log 'bridge' that was there in 2014 will have been replaced by something more substantial.

to a stream. ◀ After crossing the stream turn right and follow a pebbly road down to the river and then south, mainly along the side of river for 3km to a sign (**7**) (630m) offering two routes to Bad Tölz. Turn right and follow a path through trees and across a meadow (there is a cross in the meadow, the Seidlkreuz) to a road.

On the other side of the road follow ITV waymarks along the side of a meadow and then turn left (**8**) and cross it to a farmstead (**Lochen**) on a low hill. Pass through the farmstead and follow its access road downhill, turn right and head along a road for 800m to the hamlet of **Rimslrain** (690m).

The next stretch is somewhat tedious involving a **road walk** through rolling open countryside. For the first time however the views south to the foothills of the Alps and tomorrow's challenge are uninterrupted.

Continue south along the road for 2.4km past the hamlet of **Leitzing** and on to **Nodern**. Turn left at the road junction and then right 100m later (**9**) (ignoring cycle route signs to Bad Tölz). Take the left fork at the next junction (**10**) and head east through the hamlet of **Pröstein**. At the next junction (**11**), turn right and head into **Abberg**. As the road disappears follow a track down the hill to the main road to Bad Tölz.

Cross the main road and follow a cycle path south. After 600m drop down to the river (dammed to form a lake at this point – the **Isarstausee**) and follow a walkway for 1.8km into **Bad Tölz**.

BAD TÖLZ 645M

Bad Tölz is known for its spas and historic medieval town centre and enjoys spectacular views of the Alps. On the western bank of the Isar River lies the Kurverwaltung, or modern spa, whose iodine-rich waters are known for their soothing and healing powers. A major attraction is the Alpamare, Europe's first indoor water park with long water slides, wave pool, a surf wave, and a range of thermal outdoor pools. Another major attraction is Stadtpfarrkirche, a church built in 1466, which is an excellent example of late-Gothic architecture.

The town has all the essential services and its pedestrianised main street is full of cafés serving fabulous Bavarian cakes. For a traditional hotel close to the centre of town consider the quirky Hotel Kolbergarten (breakfast only, **www.hotel-kolbergarten.de**, tel 49 8041 78920) which has particularly wonderful rooms. Located on the main street itself and very easy to find is Posthotel Kolberbräu (**www.kolberbraeu.de**, tel 49 8041 76880). Bad Tölz has a lot of churches and the bells ring throughout the night at slightly different times on the hour and quarter hours: not a good place for light sleepers.

STAGE 3
Bad Tölz to the Tutzinger Hütte

Start	Bridge over the River Isar in the town centre (645m)
Distance	21km
Ascent/Descent	1250m/570m
Difficulty	Challenging
Walking time	7hr 40min
Maximum altitude	1712m
Refreshments	There are plenty of places to stop for refreshments.
Routefinding	Navigation is straightforward although timings on signs can be misleading.
Variants	A cable car can be taken from the Brauneck cable car station to the Brauneckhaus (saving about 750m of ascent) and the difficult walk long the Benediktenwand ridge can be avoided by taking the E4 variant.

Stage 3 is a walk of two halves. The first continues the riverside theme of the first two days and follows the now-familiar River Isar to Lenggries. The second involves the first significant climb of the whole route, including one of the most difficult stretches of the whole Traumpfad. Some experience and a head for heights are needed here and care needs to be taken in bad weather.

The Tutzinger is a popular hut and likely to be busy, so even if you've booked a room expect to share it with others. It's very friendly and in August 2015, like many huts in the Alps, it had a Nepalese chef.

From the main bridge in the centre of town, drop down to the riverside walkway/cycleway and head south along the western bank of the **River Isar**. Follow this path all the way to Lenggries. About 4km south on a bend in the river, is a 'forest' of 'Steinpyramiden' – cairns built by walkers looking for luck on the journey ahead. After another 3km the route arrives on the outskirts of **Arzbach** and the possibility of a refreshments stop. (Lenggries is still an hour away.)

Continue along the flat and well-marked path for another 3.5km to **Lenggries**.

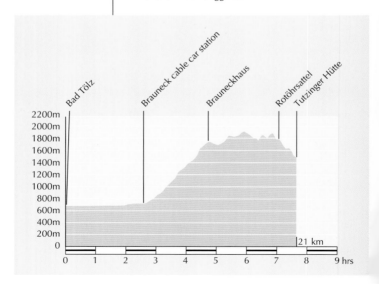

56

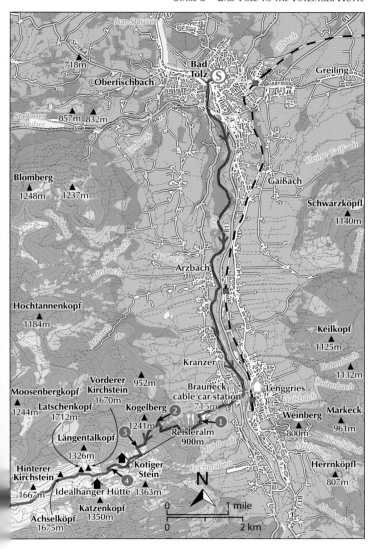

If a break is needed, turn left and head towards the centre of town and treat yourself to coffee and cake (much cheaper here than Bad Tölz). Lenggries has all the essential facilities (including a train station) and lots of accommodation. For a hotel consider the centrally located Hotel Altwirt (**www.altwirt-lenggries.de**, tel 49 8042 97320) or the Gasthof Pension Neuwirt (**www.neuwirt.info**, tel 49 8042 8943), also well located.

A restaurant near the Brauneck cable car station (715m) can provide refreshments if needed.

At the roundabout in the centre of Lenggries (with a bridge over the River Isar immediately to the east) head south along the main road taking a right hand fork after 100m and continue along the road out the village to the bottom of the cable car. ◄

From the southwest corner (**1**) of the car park near the lift climb up along a dirt road (signed 451 to Brauneck) up to a restaurant, the **Reisleralm** (900m). Just past the turn-off to the restaurant join a forest path leaving the dirt road to the right and follow it through trees. After emerging from the trees and crossing a meadow the path again joins a dirt road (**2**). Follow this across an open grassy hillside before leaving it (**3**) to join a path for the final climb to the cable car station. The **Brauneckhaus** (1540m) is just above the cable car station along the ridge to the west.

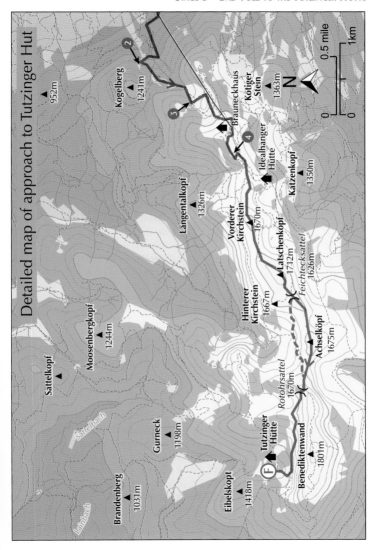

Detailed map of approach to Tutzinger Hut

59

The climb of around 800m to the Brauneckhaus is the **first significant climb** of the Munich to Venice route and getting to the top in around two hours is good going. The views are great and it's a good place to stop for lunch. It's also the first alpine club (DAV) hut on the route and offers accommodation (**www.brauneckgipfelhaus.de**, tel 49 8042 8786).

From the Brauneckhaus head west downhill along a road and continue left along a path. After 200m (**4**) the sign on the side the hill offers two routes to Tutzinger Hütte. One, the E4 variant, runs first to the south and then to the north of the main route, misses the ridge walk and is the easier of the two. The second section of the main route, after the Feichtecksattel, includes a section best left for experienced walkers.

The **views from the ridge** can be excellent. (It's a point where the meeting of warm and cold air can generate dramatic weather results.) To the north the views across German plain should include splashes of silver, reflection off the Ammersee and Stambergersee huge lakes located to the west of Munich. To the south is the northern ridge of the Karwendel, approached in two days' time, and to the east, a sharp point, the Rotwand (1884m).

The main route runs along the ridge ascending and descending a series of mini-summits. In several places there are ladders and fixed ropes (the first of many on the Traumpfad) and in other places the route is steep and exposed. The first part of the ridge, however, (over Vorderer Kirchstein (1670m) and Latschenkopf (1712m)) is much easier than the second half so the best option if you want to avoid too much exposure is to drop onto the E4 route at **Feichtecksattel** (1626m). The second half of ridge walk includes some exposed stretches, particularly on the ascent and descent of the **Achseslköpf** (1675m) and care needs to be taken.

E4 variant from Feichtecksattel
From the pass the E4 variant drops to the north side of ridge before heading west. The signs suggest that the E4 route takes 3hrs and the tougher route (marked 'Tutzinger Hütte via Acheslköpfe 451A') 1.5hrs. This exaggerates the difference but the easier route loses more altitude (200m) which has to be regained before the routes merge at the Rotöhrsattel.

In places the route is steep and exposed

From the **Rotöhrsattel** (1670m) it's an easy 45min descent down to the **Tutzinger Hütte** (1347m).

> The **Tutzinger Hütte** sits in a hollow underneath the enormous wall of the Benediktenwand. If you're lucky with the weather the sunset will change the colour of the wall from battleship grey to livid pink, an effect that lasts only minutes so be ready with your camera (**www.dav-tutzinger-huette.de**, tel 49 0175 1641690).

STAGE 4
Tutzinger Hütte to Vorderriß

Start	Tutzinger Hütte (1327m)
Distance	18km; with the Benediktenwand: 19km
Ascent/Descent	710m/1270m; with the Benediktenwand: 960m/1520m
Difficulty	Moderate
Walking time	7hr 20min; with the Benediktenwand: 8hr 50min
Maximum altitude	1564m; with the Benediktenwand: 1801m
Refreshments	Today you have to make a picnic-or-not decision. If one ration of heavy hut bread a day is as much as your system can bear then stop for lunch at Jachenau where there is traditional German gasthof.
Routefinding	Waymarking is good with all the main destinations – Glaswandscharte, Jachenau and Vorderriß – clearly marked.

After the excitement of Stage 3, Stage 4 is straightforward, a pleasant easy walk. There is, however, a lot of walking through trees and views are restricted. Much of yesterday's accumulated altitude is lost and towards the end of the day, on the final approach to Vorderriß, you face the first of many knee-crunching Traumpfad descents.

From the hut, head back to the cliffs of the **Benediktenwand** (1801m) and turn right and southwest (along the 455). The path meanders its way up the mountainside – a good warm-up. After 50min and at the highest point (1564m) there is a turn-off (**1**) to the summit of the Benediktenwand which involves an additional 250m climb.

The climb up **Benediktenwand** will take about 45 mins and if the weather is good provides excellent views in all directions. To the south is the Karwendel, to be crossed in just two days' time and to west, a huge body of water, the **Walchensee**.

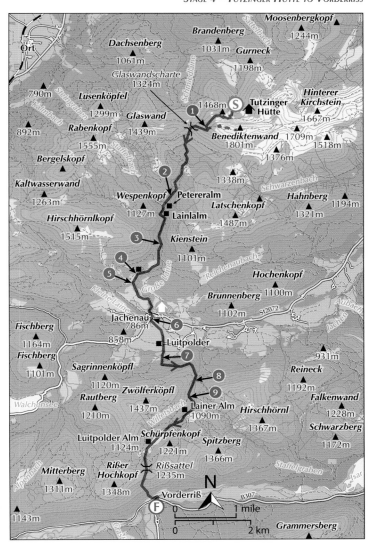

The Benediktenwand from the Tutzinger Hütte

Behind the Walchensee, in the Wetterstein mountains, is the Zugspitze, which at 2962m is Germany's highest mountain.

From the turn-off continue west along a steeply descending zig-zagging path through mixed deciduous and coniferous woodland with exposed tree roots (treacherous in the wet) and after 35min reach the **Glaswandscharte** (1324m). Turn left, head south, and continue downhill through trees crossing one then another dirt road. After about 30min a gully to the right hand side of the path will become increasingly well defined with the river at its bottom growing in size. Emerging from the trees the view of the valley opens up. After crossing a stream, descending into the main valley from the east, find the ideal place to take pictures of a waterfall (**2**) reached around 2hr 30min after leaving the hut.

Skirting round a semi-abandoned building, **Petereralm** (920m), join a dirt road on the left side of the river and follow it south. After 1km cross a bridge, pass

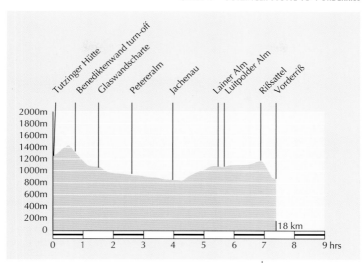

another farmstead (**Lainlalm**) and cross another bridge. Another kilometre later the route leaves the dirt road and follows a path down to a footbridge (**3**) over a river. After crossing the footbridge follow the path up through trees to a meadow, in the middle of which is an old barn (**4**). Join a dirt road heading south but leave it after 300m and turn left (**5**) onto a path that heads back to the river and down into the village of **Jachenau** (786m).

> Jachenau is a classic alpine village located in a flat-bottomed valley surrounded by mountains. It's a great place to stop for lunch and the Schuetzenhaus (closed on Wednesdays) is directly on the route. There is also accommodation in the village at the Gasthof zur Jachenau (**www.hotel-gasthof-jachenau-toelzer-land. de**, tel 49 8043 910, closed Tuesdays).

Leaving Jachenau head south along the main road. After 100m (**6**) turn left onto a path and follow it south-east across a meadow to a dirt road. Follow the dirt road

south through a farmstead (**Luitpolder** (775m)) and over a bridge across a stream. Another 50m beyond the bridge (**7**) leave the road and join a forest path and climb gently south and then east (following the 490 signs to Luitpolder Alm and Vorderriß). After a climb of 250m (and 2.5km from Jachenau) the path joins a dirt road (**8**). Continue south along the road for 300m and turn left at a junction (**9**). Follow the road into an open meadow and the **Lainer Alm** (1090m), which may be serving buttermilk, reached 90min after leaving Jachenau.

From Lainer Alm, head southwest across the meadow into trees. The **Luitpolder Alm** (1124m), another meadow among the trees, is reached after 20min. From the southwest side of this meadow join a path and continue south up through trees to the **Rißsattel** (1235m).

The views from **Rißsattel** are excellent. Directly below you running south/north, is the River Isar, stretching across an oversized gravel bed. It's a very dramatic feature which, depending on the light, will either be battleship grey or, if lucky, a bright silver.

From the pass the path zig-zags its way steeply down a grassy hillside for nearly 450m down to **Vorderriß** (792m).

66

Vorderriß (**www.post-vorderriss.de**, tel 49 80 45277), or the Gasthof Post, is the last hotel before the Austrian border and offers accommodation in rooms or small dormitories. Occasionally the rooms are full. If so and you are not prepared to stay in a dormitory, then Hinterriß, over the border and about 2hr along the road, is the next option.

STAGE 5
Vorderriß to the Karwendelhaus

Start	Gasthof Post (790m)
Distance	24km
Ascent/Descent	1050m/50m
Difficulty	Moderate
Walking time	7hr 10min
Maximum altitude	1780m
Refreshments	Hinterriß is a good place to get refreshments and prepare for the big climb of the day.
Routefinding	Although straightforward and well signed the route from Hinterriß up to the Karwendelhaus has changed recently and the printed maps have not kept pace.

Stage 5 crosses the border and enters the Karwendel National Park. The scenery is truly spectacular. Unfortunately it comes with a price with some grim road walking (albeit with good views) at the beginning.

From the Gasthof Post join the road heading south and follow it for 4.5km along a valley to the **Oswaldhütte** (850m) and the border between Germany and Austria – one country down, two to go. ▶

Continue south along the road for another 1.5km (crossing from the east to west side of the river) and leave it as it turns east towards a bridge (**1**). Follow a dirt road south, for 4.8km to **Hinterriß** (928m) reached about 2hr 30min after leaving Vorderriß.

The Oswaldhütte is a small farmhouse restaurant and the last place to get German buttermilk.

HINTERRISS 928M

Hinterriß is the gateway to the National Park and has a particularly impressive visitor centre. If you have time it's well worth the entry fee and provides interesting information on the natural and cultural history of the Karwendel area. This includes an explanation of how royal patronage encouraged the development of tourism (Queen Victoria's daughter, the Duchess of Albany, is buried here).

The visitor centre information commemorates Hermann von Barth, whose name is associated with the 'discovery' of the northern limestone alps in general and the Karwendel in particular. Numerous first ascents are credited to his short but hyperactive career of summiting and cataloguing. He was 23 when he moved to the Berchtesgaden and between May and September (1869) he climbed 49 peaks. He visited the Karwendel the following year and summited 88 peaks, many being first ascents. Initially he couldn't attract a publisher but, in 1874, his first book *Aus den Nördlichen Kalkalpen* (From the Northern Limestone Alps) appeared and quickly became a classic of German alpine literature. His work was not just a catalogue but also captured the Romantic, nostalgic and even heroic spirit so important in the alpine ideal. On his only trip away from his beloved alps, an expedition to Angola in 1876, he caught a tropical disease and, in a state of despair during a fever, shot himself in the heart.

The relationship between the alpinist ideal and the popularity of the alps has always been strained but Hermann von Barth would surely have surprised at how popular the Karwendel has become for mountain bikers. To witness this you need a sunny weekend when hundreds of cyclists head up to the Karwendelhaus (1765m) for beer and Kaiserschmarrn. People think nothing of cycling up to the pass particularly from Scharnitz – the town at the bottom of the valley to the west (off map) – leaving their bike there and then climbing up the Birkkarspitz. The road up to the Karwendelhaus is part of the Bike Trail Tirol, which at 1000km is longest mountain bike route in the Alps.

Although it's in Austria, Hinterriß can only be reached by road from Germany as Germans will tell you with great glee. As well as its excellent National Park visitor centre it also has a good hotel, the Hotel Gasthof zur Post (www.post-hinterriss.info, tel 43 5245 206), the walls of which are almost completely covered with dead animals. It is the last place to stop for food before Karwendelhaus, some 4–5hr away.

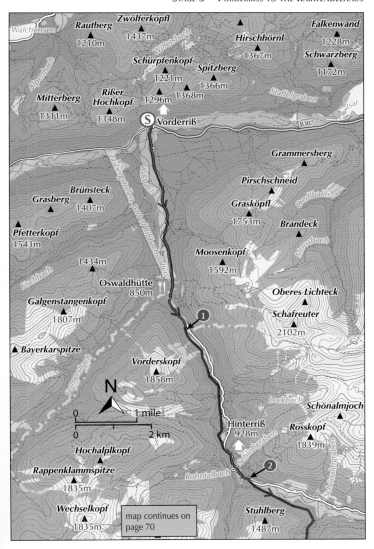

map continues on page 70

69

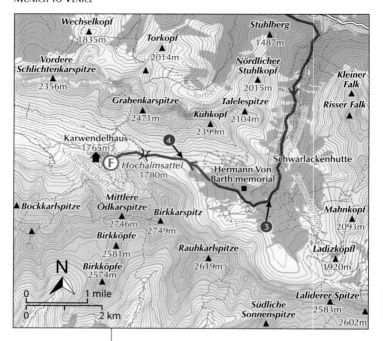

From Hinterriß, head east along the main road. On the opposite side of the road to the car park (**2**) signs point the way along a dirt road to the Karwendelhaus. After 15min turn left onto a path (well signed) and continue east. About 1.8km from Hinterriß the path swings south into a beautiful gorge, cut by a tributary to the Isar, the **Johannesbach**. Continue south through trees along the western side of the gorge.

After 800m the gorge opens up and the path crosses the river and joins a dirt road (and the Bike Trail Tirol), re-crosses the river and continues south. Perhaps in an effort to separate the bikes from walkers a path leaves the dirt road and rejoins it further along. (It does this twice.) Continue for a further 3km (on either the dirt road or the parallel running paths) to the unused **Schwarzlackenhütte**

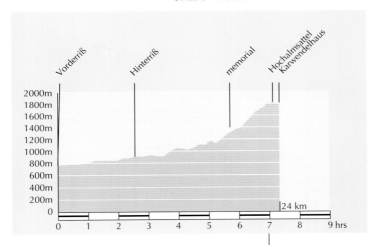

where the path crosses the river. Here the route has been subject to change but the signs direct walkers left, away from the cyclists and close to the river: follow the latest signs.

As the route progresses up the valley it enters a 'bowl' in the heart of the Karwendel and the scenery becomes ever more impressive. Immediately ahead is the spectacular main ridge of the Karwendel, a huge west/east limestone wall. An impressive series of 2500m peaks feature on the ridge the highest of which, the **Birkkarspitz**, is just around the corner.

Continue climbing up the path for 15min rejoining the cycle route and the junction (**3**) with a long-distance footpath called the 'Alderweg' (marked with eagle's wings). There are signs pointing east to the Falkenhütte. Continue in a south-southwest direction up a path looking down on a wide expanse of gravel in the valley bottom. As the route climbs away from the river it enters a relatively flat area, the Kleiner Ahornboden, consisting of alpine meadows sparsely dotted with ancient maple trees. In the middle of this flat area is a hut (1400m) and a memorial to Hermann Von Barth. The birth date on the memorial is wrong!

71

*Above the
Johannesbach
approaching the
Karwendel*

You are now well
above the treeline
and the views,
particularly east
along the main ridge,
are worth savouring.

Head past the hut in a west-northwest direction
(escaping the cyclists whose route heads south-southwest) up a shallow valley for 50min (now on the E4
alpine variant). After 300m (**4**) the path rejoins a dirt road
and the cycle path and makes the final climb to the pass,
the **Hochalmsattel** (1780m) marked with a cross. ◀

The **Karwendelhaus** (1765m) is 15min from the pass.

The Karwendelhaus (**www.karwendelhaus.com**, tel 43
720 983554), run by the Ruech family, is a wonderful place. It can get extremely busy particularly on a
sunny Sunday when it will be full of refuelling cyclists.
It also gets busy most evenings and advanced booking
is recommended if you want to avoid the dormitory.
It's a professional but friendly operation and your host
will ensure that everyone gets a weather forecast and is
briefed on local walking conditions. This is important
as tomorrow you face the Birkkarspitz.

STAGE 6
Karwendelhaus to the Hallerangerhaus

Start	Karwendelhaus (1765m)
Distance	15km; via Scharnitz: 38km
Ascent/Descent	1550m/1560m; with the Birkkarspitz: 1659m/1669m; via Scharnitz: 800m/805m
Difficulty	Challenging
Walking time	9hr
Maximum altitude	2620m; with the Birkkarspitz: 2749m; via Scharnitz: 1765m
Refreshments	There is nowhere to eat until you get to the Kastenalm, which serves buttermilk, beer, cake and cold meat, so top up on energy rations.
Routefinding	If the weather is good, navigation is very straightforward and waymarking excellent.
Variant	In bad weather to Hallerangerhaus via Sharnitz.

The Traumpfad is a great walk punctuated with days that are truly memorable and Stage 6 is definitely one of them.

However, alternative routes should be considered in bad weather and the host at the Karwendelhaus will provide up-to-date information on conditions around the pass where snow or ice can make conditions treacherous.

Having climbed all the way up to the Schlauchkarsattel, most people will want to climb Birkkarspitz itself. It involves another 130m and steel cables but the views from the top of the highest mountain in the Karwendel are excellent.

Bad weather alternative

If the weather or conditions underfoot are bad then walk down to Scharnitz, around the ridge and back along the valley to the Hallerangerhaus. Follow the signs to Scharnitz along Route 201 for 19km, descending 800m and taking around 4hr. From Scharnitz take the 224 to

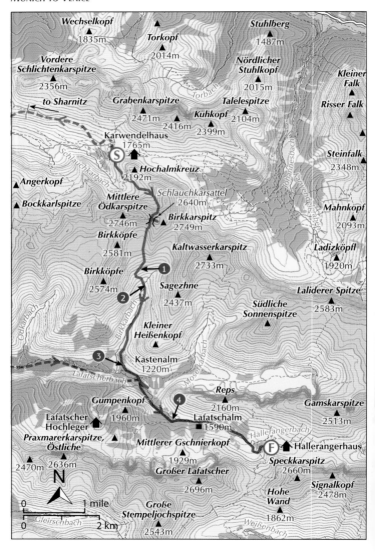

Wechselkopf
1835m

Torkopf
2014m

Stuhlberg
1487m

Vordere
Schlichtenkarspitze
2356m

Nördlicher
Stuhlkopf
2015m

Kleiner
Falk

to Sharnitz

Grabenkarspitze
2471m

Talelespitze
2104m

Risser Falk

Torbach

Kuhkopf
2416m   2399m

Karwendelhaus
1765m

Steinfalk
2348m

Schlauchkarbach

Johannesbach

Hochalmkreuz
2192m

Angerkopf

Schlauchkarsattel
2640m

Mahnkopf
2093m

Bockkarlspitze

Mittlere
Ödkarspitze
2746m

Birkkarspitz
2749m

Karwendelbach

Birkköpfe
2581m

Kaltwasserkarspitz
2733m

Ladizköpfl
1920m

Birkköpfe
2574m

①

Sagezhne
2437m

Laliderer Spitze
2583m

②

Südliche
Sonnenspitze

Ödkarbach

Kleiner
Heißenkopf

Birkkarbach

Moserkarbach

③

Lafatscherbach

Kastenalm
1220m

Reps
2160m

Gamskarspitze
2513m

Gumpenkopf

④

Lafatscher
Hochleger

1960m

Lafatschalm
1590m

Hallerangerbach

Hallerangerhaus

Praxmarerkarspitze,
Östliche

Mittlerer Gschnierkopf

Speckkarspitz
2660m

2470m   2636m

1929m

N

Großer Lafatscher
2696m

Signalkopf
2478m

Hohe
Wand
1862m

Gleirschbach

0   1 mile
0   2 km

Große
Stempeljochspitze
2543m

Weißenbach

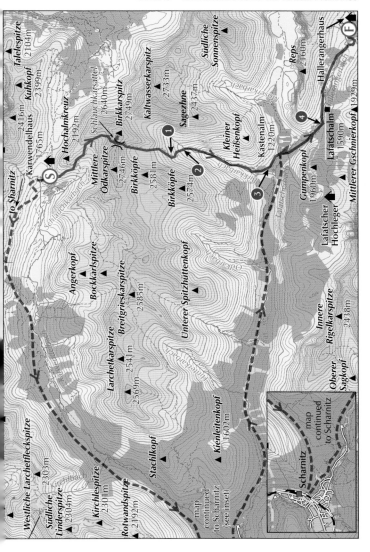

75

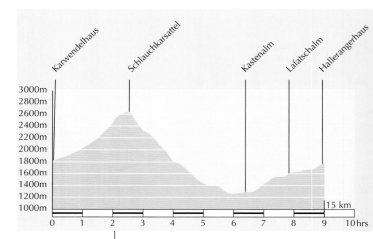

Hallerangerhaus east along the valley – another 19km walk that, with 800m of climb, will take around 5hr. There is plenty of accommodation in Scharnitz and there is the option of getting a taxi at least part of the way up the valley. It is also possible to avoid Scharnitz by leaving the 201 at Karwendelsteg and following Route 28 to the Gasthof Weisenhof where you could stay or continue on the 224 to Hallerangerhaus.

For the main route, head 100m back up the trail from the Karwendelhaus towards a building nearer the pass. Follow a steep rocky path behind the building (marked the 225) and clamber up through avalanche barriers assisted by steel cables. Past the barriers follow the path as it swings south and climbs more gently up the side of a deep valley.

The **valley** is on the north-northwestern side of the Birkkarspitz (2749m) and you will probably be in shade almost until the pass is reached. Although it may be chilly in the early morning it is a beautiful walk. Initially it follows a gentle grassy path and climbs easily around and into the valley. Dwarf pine cling to the scree but soon disappear as altitude is gained. As the path climbs it enters an increasingly barren grassless landscape where chamois or ibex miraculously find something to eat.

After two hours of steady climbing the path swings west towards the pass. North-facing patches of snow linger in the shade for most of the summer. As the pass gets closer the path becomes less defined and is probably subject to change. Occasional small bits of rock, loosened as the sun warms the mountain, may become dislodged. The final haul to the pass, the **Schlauchkarsattel** (2640m), is particularly steep.

The **pass** is a convenient point to stop, relax and perhaps grab a well-deserved bite to eat. The climb up to the top of the Birkkarspitz, past a little refuge where some enterprising souls may well have spent the night, will take no more than 15min.

From summit, looking north is the northern Karwendel chain (a line of 2500m peaks) and beyond that the Benediktenwand and the German plain. To the east along the main Karwendel ridge the sharp summit of the Kaltwasserkarspitze (2733m) is particularly prominent. To the south and across the valley lie the Gleiersch-Halltal mountains the highest peak in which is the **Große Lafatscher** (2696m), the fifth highest mountain in the Karwendel and the highest not in the central chain. Beyond Gleiersch-Halltal, and on the horizon, are the mountains of the main Alpine ridge. The distinct white feature is the Hintertux glacier. To the west, beyond the arid limestone of the main ridge, is the Wetterstein and Germany's highest mountain, the Zugspitze.

The first 30m of descent from the pass is the most demanding. Judged not difficult enough to warrant steel cables it is still very steep. Steel cables then kick in and

Cable-assisted
descent from the
Schlauchkarsattel

The icy cold water
will provide instant
refreshment for
feet hammered
by the descent.

continue for 150m or so, one of the most sustained
stretches of cabling on the whole Traumpfad. After you
have clambered down over all those rocks the path
changes character to descend down a steep scree field.
Super-confident walkers will be tempted to scree run.

The path now heads south down a valley, into the
sun on a good day, with huge cliffs on either side. This
is a stunning stretch of walking, and if you haven't had
something to eat at the pass, there are some perfect picnic spots. The first (**1**), about halfway down, is on top of a
small rise in the middle of the valley and the second (**2**)
(1736m), shortly afterwards, is by a stream. ◄

The descent from the pass to the stream will take
around 2hr. Next, follow a well-defined path on the eastern side of the valley through pine, initially dwarf then
larger, down to the bottom and into a large east-west running valley. Continue along the valley floor through trees
to a junction (**3**) with a dirt road where a sign indicates
that the Hallerangerhaus is 2hr away. Follow the dirt road
(Route 225) east. After 300m the route leaves it and heads

south to where signs invite a visit to **Kastenalm** (1220m) (about 300m away) a traditional farmhouse serving beer, buttermilk, cold meat and cake.

From the turnoff to Kastenalm head southeast along a forest road and climb up through trees. Ignore a turnoff (**4**) to the **Lafatscher Hochleger** hut (after 55min walk and a climb of 280m).

On the hillside to the north mounds of spoil are evident, these date back to an old **silver mine** which, amongst others in the Karwendel, employed thousands of miners in the 16th century.

Continuing up through trees the route emerges into the **Lafatschalm** (1590m), a classic alpine meadow complete with an ancient geranium-bedecked chalet. Directly ahead, at the end of the valley, is the **Speckkarspitz** (2660m). The **Hallerangerhaus** (1768m), with its DAV club flag clearly visible ahead, and you should reach it 40min later.

You have two accommodation options. The Hallerangerhaus (**www.hallerangerhaus.at**, tel 43 72034 7028), the Alpine Club hut, and the Halleranger Alm (**www.halleranger-alm.at**, tel 43 664 1055955). Both offer accommodation in dormitories and rooms.

HALLERANGERHAUS TO THE INN VALLEY

On the approach to Laftcherjoch

Stage 7 completes the traverse of the Karwendel and descends into the Inn Valley. There are two alternative ways across the Inn Valley, however, via Hall or via Wattens a town a few kilometres to the east.

Overall the best route in terms of scenery is via Hall. From Hall the route goes to the Glungezer Hütte. After Glungezer it follows a spectacular ridge walk to Lizumer Hütte along the main ridge of the Tux Alps. It's a great stretch of walking but one that should be avoided if the weather is bad. If poor weather is anticipated then the Wattens route provides a better alternative.

The climb out of the Inn Valley via Hall is long and steep. If walkers are not worried about completing every step of the way to Venice this can be avoided by taking the chairlift part of the way up the side of the valley.

Taken together these considerations generate two main alternative ways across the Inn Valley.

- Walk down to Hall, stay there and walk up the Glungezer Hütte next day (Stage 7A).
- Walk down to Wattens stay there and then walk to the Lizumer Hütte next day (which saves a day on the overall schedule) (Stage 7B).

There is a choice of accommodation in both Hall and Wattens although Hall is the prettier town.

A third option might be to overshoot Hall by two hours and stay at Tulfes (plenty of accommodation) to take the pressure off the tough walk up to Glungezer Hütte on Stage 8.

There is also another hut on the south side of the Inn Valley, the Voldertalhütte, reached via Hall, and it is possible to go from there to Lizumer Hütte. This bad weather alternative has not been walked by the author and is not described here.

STAGE 7A
Hallerangerhaus to Hall

Start	The Hallerangerhaus (1768m)
Distance	14km
Ascent/Descent	240m/1450m
Difficulty	Moderate
Walking time	4hr 30min
Maximum altitude	2081m
Refreshments	For a mid-morning stop visit the restaurant at St Magdalena

From the Hallerangerhaus rejoin the 224 and follow the sign to the Laftcherjoch. The path climbs quickly, initially approaching cliffs on the northwest flank of the **Speckkarspitze** (2660m) before swinging west across scree and dwarf pine. It's a good path and in places bits of engineering suggest that it was built to support mining activity.

After 45min the path reaches a cross (**1**) (1985m) and from there climbs more gently up to **Laftcherjoch**

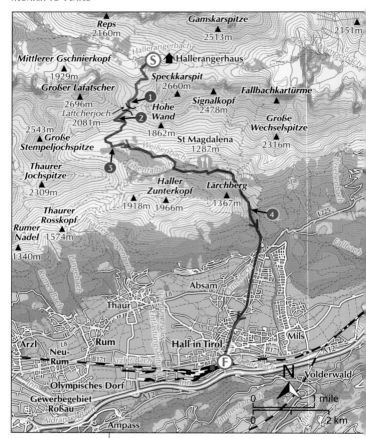

(2081m). This is your final climb in the Karwendel and rewards with good views south across the Inn Valley to the Tux Alps.

From the pass follow the path (now the 223) south-west down to junction with the 222 (**2**). Continue with the 223 heading downhill and west and soon reaching another junction (**3**) with signs to St Magdalena along the

Hirschbadsteig. Unless the weather is very bad, follow this route and head down across an open meadow and through a wooded valley to **St Magdalena** (1287m). ▶

> Most of the original **monastery of St Magdalena** was destroyed in an earthquake in the 17th century but the church and an attached gasthof remain. Now owned by the local council there is a restaurant there but currently no accommodation. It's a pretty location and a popular destination for local hikers.

Head directly east from the church and follow a path across the edge of a field into trees. Continue east along for 800m eventually dropping down to a road. Instead of joining the road (although the road is an option in bad weather) continue on the path that runs above it and stay on it as it swings south with the valley. Continue with the path for about 2km (ignoring a junction at 1.4km (**4**) where the route to Wattens goes off) until it drops down to the road and follows it into **Hall** (570m).

The bad weather alternative, which is longer, follows a mountain road (Route 221) south, past some old salt mines, before turning east to arrive at the same destination.

The cobbled streets of Hall

Hall in Tirol is a medium-sized town with several accommodation options. Good value with a traditional beer cellar is provided at the Goldener Engl (**www.goldener-engl.at**, tel 43 5223 54 6 21) located to the south of the main shopping area and near the castle. Alternatively, just to the south of the town, the Gasthof Badl (**www.badl.at/en**, tel 43 5223 56784), another traditional Austrian hotel, is directly on the route of tomorrow's walk.

STAGE 7B

Hallerangerhaus to Wattens

Start	The Hallerangerhaus (1765m)
Distance	19km
Ascent/Descent	140m/1460m
Difficulty	Moderate
Walking time	6hr 10min
Maximum altitude	2081m
Refreshments	For a mid-morning stop visit the restaurant at St Magdalena and food can also be found at Gnadenwald

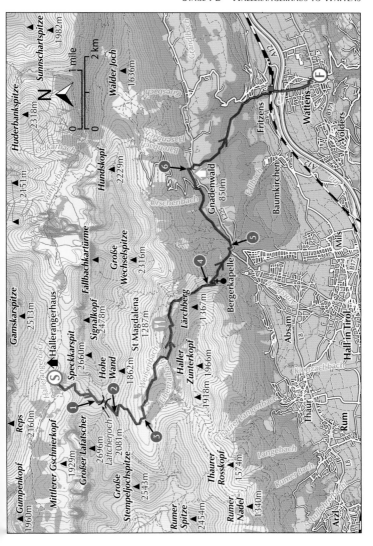

85

Approaching the Hallerangerhaus

Follow the route description in Stage 7A as far as (**4**). At this junction, take a sharp left turn down to the road. Head north along the road towards the Bergerkapelle and take a right turn just before you reach the chapel to follow a path southeast, across a stream and onto a dirt road. Follow this dirt road southeast for a kilometre to a junction with other paths (**5**).

Head east and follow the signs pointing along the Besinnungsweg to Gnadenwald. Continue for 2.6km (watch out for the Jakobsweg signs – last seen on the first stage of the Traumpfad), past a range of information boards and 'interesting objects'. Pass to the north of a church (St Martin's) and 300m later (**6**) turn right and head down to a road running through the dispersed settlement of **Gnadenwald** (850m)

The Gasthof Martinsstuben (**www.martinsstuben.at**, tel 43 5223 52501), just along the road to the right, provides refreshments and accommodation.

Cross the road, turn left and after 50m turn right and follow signs pointing to Fritzens along a path past an equestrian centre, where, if you're lucky, you will see

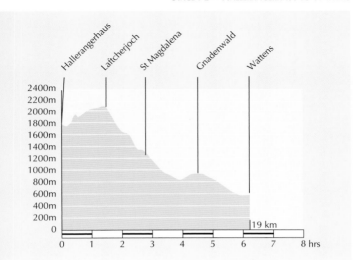

horses doing dressage. After 300m the path joins a gravel road from the west (coming down from the Gasthof Martinsstuben) and follows it southeast 2.3km through

The descent to Wattens

meadows to **Fritzens**. Once in Fritzens head down the main road to the railway station, and cross the bridge over the Inn to **Wattens**.

WATTENS 550M

Wattens is a small industrial town on the south bank of the Inn. As well as massive mill making paper for cigarettes (seen just after crossing the bridge) the town is also home to the Swarovski glass-cutting factory and Crystal Worlds visitor centre, where most of the residents work.

For accommodation consider the four-star Hotel Goldener Adler (**www.goldener-adler-wattens.at**, tel 43 5224 52255) in the centre of town or, just to the east of the Adler, the Pension Clara (**www.pension-clara.at**, tel 43 5224 52151)

2 INN VALLEY
TO PFUNDERS

Looking east to the Hintertux (Stage 9)

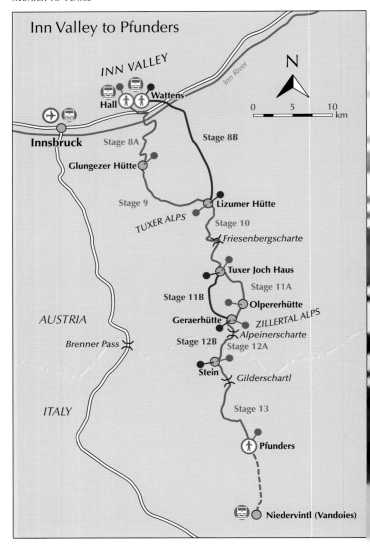

Looking back across the Inn Valley to the Karwendel (Stage 8A)

In the second section of the Traumpfad you tick off some significant milestones. Firstly the route crosses the Alpine core, the geological heart of the Alps. Secondly it crosses the watershed: the divide between rivers flowing north then east into the Danube and the Black Sea, and rivers flowing south into the Adriatic and the Mediterranean. Thirdly it enters the south Tyrol and Italy. Subtle changes start to emerge in the local cuisine and there are pronounced and confusing changes to the naming conventions, with nouns expressed in German, Italian or even a local language, Ladin.

Section 2 is spectacular. Depending on whether you choose to go via the Glungezer Hütte or the Lizumer Hütte the mountain traverse stays at over 2000 metres for four or five days. The route crosses two mountain groups – the Tux and the Zillertal Alps. The Tux are the gentle ones (sometimes disparagingly described as pre-Alps). They are more rounded, without the huge peaks and glaciers of their cousins to the south. The walking is superb and the long 'ridge' from the Glungezer to the Lizumer hut is definitely a candidate for the best day of the whole of the Munich to Venice route.

The Zillertal Alps, themselves positioned immediately to the west of the huge Hohe Tauern range, are definitely more dramatic. You reach them on Stage 11 just to the north of the Hintertux Glacier (famous as a year-round ski resort) when the trail crosses a high pass, the Friesenbergscharte (confusingly part of ridge known as the Tux Crest). After the pass you drop down to a spectacular valley side path which is followed all the way to a pass and the Italian border before a final descent to Stein. After viewing the

91

Hochfeiler (3510m), the highest peak of the range, and its glacier from a distance the route then gets much closer, crosses another pass, the Gliderschartl (2644m) before heading down the beautiful Pfunders valley.

The biggest challenge involves crossing the Tux Crest. The standard itinerary involves a steep descent from a pass, the Friesenbergscharte assisted by fixed steel cables. The alternative route, via the Geraerhütte involves crossing the crest via a pass known as the Alpeinerscharte which doesn't involve fixed steel cables but does require a similar head for heights. Both routes are about as challenging as the descent from the Birkkarspitz in Section 1.

ACCESS AND ACCOMMODATION

Niedervintl (Vandoies), a 20min early morning bus ride away from Pfunders, has a train station and is a good exit point. If leaving the trail you could finish your walk at Pfunders and still head home early the next day. Niedervintl has a good train service with frequent trains to Munich (taking about four hours) and buses to Innsbruck (taking about an hour).

This are lots of huts on this stretch of the Traumpfad, the facilities at the Lizumer Hütte and Olpererhütte being particularly good. The guest house at Stein is fairly basic but homely, and the small hotel at Pfunders is also very comfortable.

KEY INFORMATION

Distance	91km (or 71km via Stage 8B and skipping Stage 9)
Total ascent	10,760m
Total descent	8880m
Alternative schedule	The standard itinerary (described in Stages 11A and 12A) involves walking across some ugly ski runs near the Hintertux glacier and the route via the Geraerhütte (Stages 11B and 12B) is a good alternative. This section can be shortened by a day by taking a chairlift from below the Tuxer Joch Haus up to the Tuxer Ferner Haus and combining Stages 11A and 12A. The alternatives are discussed as part of the introduction to Stages 11 and 12.

STAGE 8A
Hall to the Glungezer Hütte

Start	Goldener Engl Gasthof, Hall (570m)
Distance	22km: via cable car: 18km
Ascent/Descent	2400m/450m; via cable car: 960m/1540m
Difficulty	Moderate
Walking time	8hr 50min; via cable car: 6hr 30min
Maximum altitude	2610m
Refreshments	Happily there are plenty of places to stop for refreshments. The Tulfein Alm is particularly well positioned at the start of the final climb to the Glungezer Hütte although it's a popular destination for local walkers and on a sunny day service can be very slow.

There is no getting away from it, walking up from Hall to the Glungezer Hütte, a climb of 2400m, is a slog and will take most people 9hr. The most popular German guide to the Traumpfad assumes walkers take the lift and, although this doesn't seem right on a 'walk' from Munich to Venice, it is understandable. The lifts carrying day hikers up to beautiful walks around the Tulfein Alm are a tempting alternative way up particularly if time is precious. It is however 'doable' on foot and you have to get there somehow to experience the delights of Stage 9, from the Glungezer Hütte to the Lizumer Hütte.

The walk itself can be broken down into three parts: the initial climb out of the valley through a series of hillside villages; a section where the route zig-zags its way across a long piste and underneath chairlifts; and a final unavoidable climb up to the Glungezer Hütte itself. If the weather is good the progressively improving views of the Karwendel will at least be a partial reward for all the hard work.

On the southeast side of the main junction in the middle of Hall, near the Goldener Engl Gasthof, is a castle and a small park. ▶ Head south through the park, turn left past the castle, and then right onto the Münzergasse. After about 100m, turn left and pass through a subway

The castle is home to one of Europe's oldest mints.

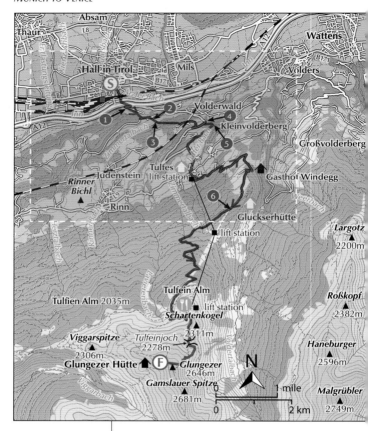

On the other side of the footbridge there is a Munich to Venice information board.

underneath a railway line. Turn right and then left after a few metres to cross a footbridge over the Inn. ◄

Turn left past the Gasthof Badl, follow the road underneath the autobahn and take the first turn right. After about 100m (**1**) leave the road, turn right onto a footpath and follow it southeast up through trees arriving at another road after about 500m. Turn left to head east down to a small settlement and before leaving the

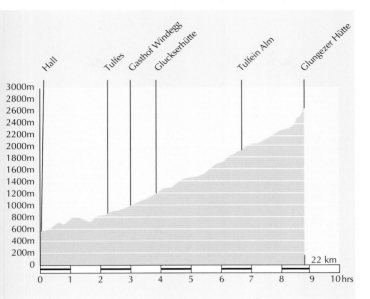

Hall · Tulfes · Gasthof Windegg · Glückserhütte · Tulfein Alm · Glungezer Hütte

22 km

settlement (**2**) take a right hand turn onto an agricultural road heading south through a meadow. After 100m take a left turn at a fork (**3**) following the sign to Tulfes and head east through trees reaching a road and another small village after 800m. (The railway line marked on the map at this point is in a tunnel here.)

Turn left and follow a road downhill to a junction with a larger road. Turn left onto the larger road and follow it northeast for 400m (**4**). Turn right onto a forest trail and follow it east for 200m before taking an easily-missed turn (**5**) onto a forest path heading south and then southwest. Follow the path along the side of a valley through trees and across meadows until it emerges near a large house onto a road. Follow the road south to the village of **Tulfes** (925m) where you can get refreshments and, if you have had a change of heart, catch a lift up to the Tulfein Alm.

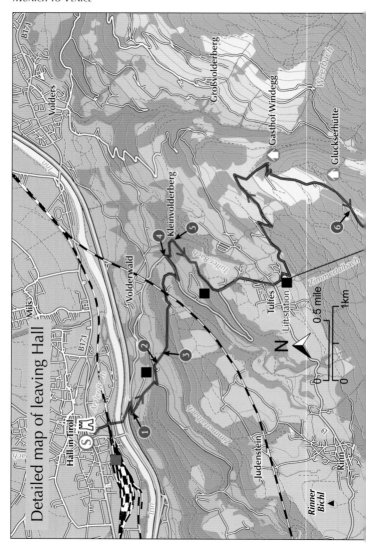

Detailed map of leaving Hall

For the **chairlift**, walk down to the lift station about 100m south of the main road near a large car park. After a change at the Halsmarter Gasthof, the lift arrives at top station (2020m) from where it's a short walk to the Tulfein Alm.

Tulfes is a ski resort with accommodation. Directly on the route is the Hotel Pension Glungezer (**www.glungezer.net**, tel 43 5223 78302) but the Gasthof Neuwirt (**www.neuwirt-tulfes.at**, tel 43 5223 78309) is also nearby.

Leave the main road in the centre of Tulfes, head south to the chairlift and follow a quiet road climbing gently east. After 2km (and some zig-zags) the road swings south and past a shingled wooden chapel and the **Gasthof Windegg** (1190m) (accommodation available, tel 43 5223 78313).

Just beyond the Gasthof Windegg take a left-hand fork and continue south for 1.5km to the **Glucserhütte** restaurant (1255m). Continue past the Glucserhütte and after passing through a gate join a dirt road (**6**). Here there are direct and less direct options. The shortest and most painful follows a linear clearing on the left (soon turning into a piste) directly up the hill to the **Tulfein Alm** (2035m). The friendlier option continues along the dirt road and Route 37 on a more meandering journey to the same destination. Either way the Tulfein Alm, reached after about 2hr 30min and 600m of climb is an ideal place to stop and have a break.

Now well above the treeline the **final stage** to the Glungezer Hütte starts to feel, once again, like real alpine walking. With any luck the views north to the Karwendel should uninterrupted and spectacular, something to savour for the last two hours of the climb.

Follow the path from behind the Tulfein Alm south before swinging east along a dirt road up the side of a

Glungezer Hütte

valley. As the dirt road turns south again, and heads up to a pass, the **Tulfeinjoch** (2278m), the route turns onto a path, well marked but passing through a rocky and sparse terrain. Continue south, climbing all the time as an increasingly steep path swings west and zigs-zags its way up to a ridge. Apart from the cable for the supply lift there is no sign of the **Glungezer Hütte** (2610m) which is on the other side of the ridge and hidden amongst the boulders.

Once reached the Glungezer Hütte is surprisingly nice. Although short on facilities (limited water and no shower) it's a friendly place to stay with great views. The quality of the food, produced by a couple of Nepalese cooks, is really good (**www.glungezer.at**, tel 43 5223 78018).

STAGE 8B

Wattens to the Lizumer Hütte

Start	Hotel Goldener Adler, Wattens (550m)
Distance	17km
Ascent/Descent	1760m/210m
Difficulty	Moderate
Walking time	7hr 40min
Maximum altitude	2020m
Refreshments	There are a couple of places to stop along the way for lunch and the Gasthof Säge is particularly good.

The walk up the valley from Wattens to the Lizumer Hütte is best described as pleasant rather than exciting and, although it's a gentle way to complete a 1400m climb, missing it would not a great loss.

Initially on the side of the valley the route passes through old farming villages, some of which now have a suburban feel. It drops down, tracking a river through conifers, before climbing into an open alpine landscape and then making the final approach to the Lizumer Hütte.

From the centre of Wattens, near the Hotel Goldener Adler, head west and take the first right south down the Lange Gasse. Follow the road for 500m (**1**), then joining a path climbing south as the road turns east. The path is signed to the Lager Walchen and initially follows a route marked by the 14 stations of the cross (a series of images depicting Jesus Christ on the day of his crucifixion).

Continue climbing along the path through trees for 25min until the path meets a road (**2**). Here the signs are confusing but cross the main road, join a smaller road on the other side, walk up this smaller road for a few metres and turn right and head south. If you've gone the right away, about 50m on the left there should be a small wooden chapel (**3**). About 250m further on take a left hand fork (**4**) and continue south along a path across a

A pathside station of the cross

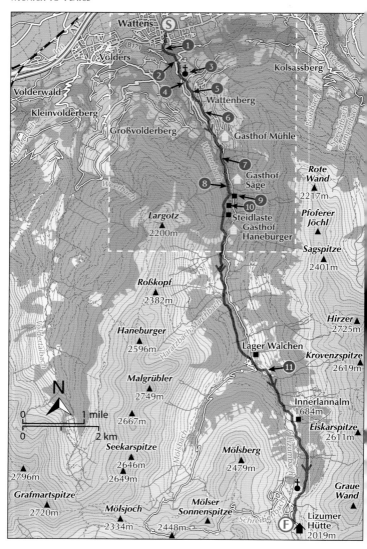

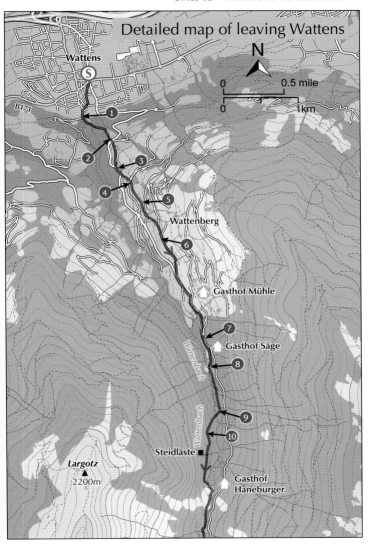

Detailed map of leaving Wattens

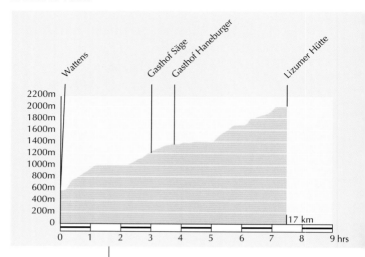

meadow. Follow this for 300m to a road (**5**) where you turn right to follow it for 300m and then left onto another path (**6**). The path continues southeast for 400m (crossing a road on the way) and joins another road. Continue along this road for 1.2km to the **Gasthof Mühle** (1010m – only open during the day for food on Friday, Saturday and Sunday.

The signs at the Gasthof Mühle are confusing. Ignore the sign to Vögelsburg and continue along the road for another 500m and then turn right (**7**) turn down to **Gasthof Säge** (1015m).

Situated in the bottom of the valley next to a saw mill (*säge* means saw) the Gasthof Säge (tel 43 5224 53173) provides accommodation as well as excellent food, and is a good place for a lunch break.

The route now runs along the bottom of the narrow valley of the **Wattenbach** through pine trees. Follow a dirt road south past the sawmill next to the Gasthof Säge taking a right hand turn at a fork 300m later (**8**). Continue along the dirt road that turns into a path (occasionally a little difficult to follow due to forestry work and poor maintenance) for 1.3km until it reaches a forestry building (**9**). Again the signs are a little obscure but below the building is a bridge (in a poor state of repair). Cross the bridge and head up the side of the valley and across a meadow to some wooden farm buildings (**10**) and follow a farm road south, past more wooden buildings, down to another bridge.

(Very) wet weather alternative
If the weather is wet (and this might be one of the reasons this option has been chosen) this part of the route can be particularly sodden. Instead of heading down to the bridge at (**9**) cross the ground immediately to its south to

A footpath through forestry – tricky when wet

join the road and follow it for 500m, then turning rig
and following a dirt road down to the next bridge.

Main route continues

◄ Stay on the west side of the river and follow the pat
climbing a little into meadows, south for another 400m
a farmstead (**Steidlaste**) to where it joins a dirt road. If yc
need refreshments, follow the dirt road over a bridge an
down to the **Gasthof Haneburger** (1410m) (tel 43 522
53875) which offers both food and accommodation.

The main route stays on the west side of the river
but in **poor weather** it may be better to avoid the
forest path, cross the bridge and walk for 1.8km
down the road to Lager Walchen.

Follow the path west away from the river before
swings south again emerging at **Lager Walchen** afte
about 30min.

This marks the entry point to the **military exercise
area** and is defined by a checkpoint (you don't need
to stop) and various military buildings. Signs warn
you against taking photographs or painting pictures.

Head south between the buildings and, after 200m
leave the dirt road and join a path to the left (**11**). The sig
points to the Lizumer Hütte and the route you're taking
called the Zirbenweg.

After running alongside trees and a meadow (and
stream), the path heads up into pine forest and stays i
the trees (climbing all the time) for about 30min. It the
emerges into a lovely upland meadow, the **Innerlannaln**
(1684m), where at last it escapes the confines of the va
ley and trees.

If the weather is good the views are excellent. You
are surrounded by the mountains of the **Tux Alps**.
Immediately to the east, marked by a series of little
rocky peaks is the Eiskarspitz (2611m) and further
north, on the same ridge, the Hirzer (2725m). To

the south and approached on the next stage is the Lizumer Reckner (2886m) and the mountain on the western side of the valley is the Mölsberg (2479m).

From the Innerlannalm it takes about an hour to get to the **Lizumer Hütte** (2019m). Continue south along the Zirbenweg climbing with the valley along a lovely path through dwarf pine. After 40min the route passes east of a chapel and another military camp.

The Lizumer Hütte (**www.glungezer.at**, tel 43 664 647 5353) has a lovely location next to a small lake surrounded by a semi-circle of mountains. It has recently been modernised and is a comfortable hut with relatively good facilities. Despite its remote location, a table in the bar/restaurant is reserved for 'locals' who eat there every night. The hut shares a website with the Glungezer Hütte and both have a policy of asking for an advance deposit by bank transfer – but if you contact them directly they will let you off!

STAGE 9
Glungezer Hütte to the Lizumer Hütte

Start	Glungezer Hütte (2610m)
Distance	15km
Ascent/Descent	750m/1330m
Difficulty	Challenging
Walking time	8hr 40min
Maximum altitude	2796m
Refreshments	Stock up on emergency rations or organise a picnic at the Glungezer Hütte (they expect you to), as there is nowhere to stop en route.
Routefinding	Although the path is reasonably well defined finding it in the rain or, worse, snow could be a real challenge and the general consensus is that the route should be avoided in bad weather.

The walk from the Glungezer to Lizumer Hütte is spectacular and a candidate for the best on the Traumpfad traverse. It's a high-altitude walk, never dropping below 2000m, and involves climbing six mini-summits, the highest of which, Rosenjoch, is 2796m. The first half of the walk is tough and although there are several short stretches of fixed cables it's the terrain rather than the climbing that slows down the pace.

Follow the signs to the Lizumer Hütte (marked Route 335) southeast towards the top of the supply lift and the first mini-summit, the **Glungezer** (2646m).

As well as a cross, the **summit** plays host to a communication equipment box the size of a shipping container. There is also a plaque to the 1964 crash of a British Eagle passenger plane which hit the mountain on the way into Innsbruck with the loss of all on board (83 people).

Continue south-southeast along the ridge to the next fairly inconspicuous summit, the **Gamslauerspitze** (2681m), reached after another 40min of walking. After

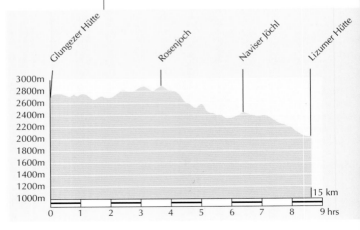

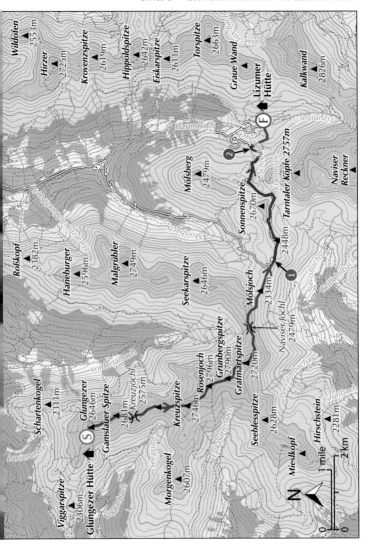

Below, to the west, are a number of little glacial lakes together known as the Seegrube.

a challenging descent down to a pass, the **Kreuzjöchl** (2575m), the route climbs up to the third mini-summit, the **Kreuzspitze** (2746m). ◄

From the Kreuzspitze it's another 50min to the highest point on the walk, the **Rosenjoch** (2796m), reached with the help of some fixed cables. Fixed cables also feature in a steep descent and the last two summits, the **Grunbergspitze** (2790m) and the **Grafmartspitze** (2720m) are easier by comparison. From the Grafmartspitze the route descends down to the grassy pass, the **Naviser Jöchl** (2479m), which marks the end of the difficult walking and is a good place to make a lunch stop.

The **views** from the ridge are excellent and a constant distraction. These include the last chance to see, the northwest, Germany's highest mountain, the Zugspitz (2962m), the Birkkarspitz hidden amongst the Karwendel to the north, and to the southwest Italy and the Brenner Pass. Ahead, dominating views for the next two days, is the Hintertux Glacier, the Olperer (3476m) and Gefrorene-Wand-Spitzen (3250m).

Looking east to Hintertux

Lizumer Hütte

From the pass the 327 continues along the southern flank of the Sonnenspitz (2670m) eventually joining a military road. ▸ A military post (**1**), providing potential shelter, is reached 50min after leaving the pass. Leave the road and join a path behind the military post, taking a direct route down to the road below. Continue down to a lake, the **Klammsee**, where, if you're desperate for a wash after the lack of a shower at the Glungezer Hütte, you could take a chilly dip. Otherwise stay on the road now swinging north then east down into a valley at the bottom of which sits the **Lizumer Hütte** (2019m). After passing through some agricultural buildings turn left onto an easily missed path (**2**) and take a more direct route than the road down across meadows to the hut below.

The route has now entered the military training area.

The Lizumer Hütte (**www.glungezer.at**, tel 43 664 647 5353) has a lovely location next to a small lake surrounded by a semi-circle of mountains. It has recently been modernised and is a comfortable hut with relatively good facilities. Despite its remote location, a table in the bar/restaurant is reserved for 'locals' who eat there every night. The hut shares a website with the Glungezer Hütte and both have a policy of asking for an advance deposit by bank transfer – but if you contact them directly they will let you off!

STAGE 10
Lizumer Hütte to the Tuxer Joch Haus

Start	Lizumer Hütte (2019m)
Distance	10km
Ascent/Descent	1140m/870m
Difficulty	Challenging
Walking time	6hr 30min
Maximum altitude	2745m
Refreshments	There is nowhere to stop for provisions, so take a packed lunch.

Stage 10 completes the Tux Alps traverse and, with the last views of the limestone mountains to north, says a final farewell to the Karwendel Alps and hello to Zillertal Alps.

This is a lovely walk involving a series of fairly distinct phases. The first is an early morning climb up the valley and over the Geierjoch (2743m); the second is a gentle contour around the head of a valley (featuring a steely glacial lake) to a second pass, the Gschützspizsattel (2657m); the third is a crashing switchback descent along a grassy mountainside down a valley bedecked with waterfalls; and finally there's a climb up to the Tuxer Joch Haus rewarded with great views of the Hintertux Glacier, the Olperer (3476m) and Gefrorene-Wand-Sptizen (3250m).

Despite a steep descent, there are no difficult sections. The manager at the Lizumer Hütte will advise on conditions if there is a lot of snow.

You will probably be accompanied by the walkers you shared breakfast with as an eagerness to get started today means everyone leaving at the same time.

From the Lizumer Hütte follow the path south (marked 323 and 'Traumpfad München-Venedig').

If the weather is good the path should be visible all the way up to the Geierjoch. Crossing an upland alpine meadow usually full of grazing cows and patches of alpenrose the only thing you need to do for the next couple of hours is reconnect the rarely active electric cattle fences. ◄

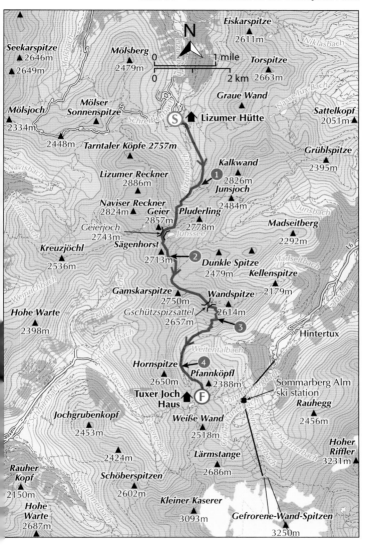

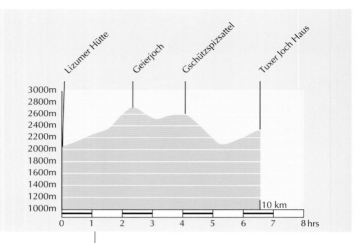

After 30min the path reaches a junction (**1**) with a path heading east (the 322 for Junsjoch) where you continue south. After another 20min it crosses a stream at the bottom of the valley and starts to climb up north-facing scree, where patches of snow can linger until late in the year, to climb up to the pass. To the west of the pass is the Lizumer Reckner (2886m) and Geier (2857m) and to the east Pluderling (2778m). After 2hr 15min from the hut you should be on the pass, the **Geierjoch** (2743m).

The **views** are tremendous. Immediately to the south is an east-facing glacial bowl containing a lake – the Junssee – a beautiful splash of colour in an otherwise grey landscape. To the east, in the distance, are the Hohe Tauern (which includes Austria's highest mountain, the Grossglockner at 3798m) and Kitzbühl Alps; to the south, beyond the bowl and the Gschützspizsattel, is the confusingly-named Tux Crest in the Zillertal Alps and its main summit the Olperer (3476m). To the north down the Lizumer Valley you can enjoy the final glimpses of the Karwendel.

The Junssee from below the Geierjoch

Head south from the pass on a descending path on the eastern side of the ridge. Continue on the 323 signed to Tuxer Joch Haus ignoring turn-offs (**2**) marked 35 to Stoankasern. The path swings to the east. If the weather is good the Gschützspizsattel should be clearly visible ahead. ▶ It takes about 1hr 50min to get from the Geierjoch to the **Gschützspizsattel** (2657m).

The descent from the pass is steep and remorseless. The path, carved into the grassy flank, zig-zags its way down into the valley, the Weitental, for 650m. On the other side of the valley (which defines the end of the Tux Alps and the beginning of the Zillertal Alps) the road up to the Tuxer Joch Haus should be clearly visible.

This initial steep descent done, for the first hundred metres or so the path heads southwest descending gently along an easy trail, very pretty with a lovely view of the **Wandspitze**. After 30min it reaches a junction with Route 31 (to Hintertux) (**3**), carries on along the 323 and starts its switchback descent in earnest. As the lower parts of the path are reached the huge waterfalls descending from the ridge become apparent.

There may well be a large patch of snow immediately below, which some walkers cross, but the safer option is on its eastern side.

At the bottom of the valley the path joins a dirt road that climbs easily up the valley. A turn-off for a short-cut (**4**), poorly signed and easily missed, is reached after about 25min. Turn left off the road to cross the stream and cutting off a corner of road-walking. The path then rejoins the road and follows it up to the **Tuxer Joch Haus**.

The Tuxer Joch Haus (2316m) (**www.tuxerjochhaus. at**, tel 43 5287 87216) is an Alpine Club Hut but has been run by the same family (who built it and sold it to the Alpine Club) for more than a hundred years. It's a busy hut and run in an efficient and very businesslike way. (Extra coffee in the morning has to be paid for!) Dormitory accommodation is usually the only option. It has a lovely sun lounge with views of the Hintertux Glacier, the Olperer and Gefrorene-Wand-Sptizen. Booking this hut is a pain – they insist on a deposit and the cheapest option from the UK is to send cash by post.

If you're happy to use ski lifts and the weather is good you might consider pressing on and **crossing the Friesenbergscharte** (2094m) today. Below the pass, on the other side, is the Friesenberghaus. Aiming for there would add another 3hr to this stage.

TUXER JOCH HAUS TO STEIN

Tuxer Joch Haus

If time needs to be saved, and you're a strong walker, the next two stages (both of which feature excellent walking) can be merged into one. Stage 11A and 12A could take 12 hours but this can be shortened by an hour by taking the ski lift and by 40 mins by staying at the Pfitscher Joch Haus instead of Stein (and bypassing Stein at the start of Stage 13). For the ski lift, walk down to Sommarberg Alm and catch the lift up to Tuxer Ferner Haus and rejoin the route just below it at the Spannagelhaus.

Stages 11B and 12B are alternatives to Stages 11A and 12A and are designed to avoid the scarred landscape of a ski resort in the summer.

STAGE 11A
Tuxer Joch Haus to the Olpererhütte

Start	Tuxer Joch Haus (2315m)
Distance	11km
Ascent/Descent	1100m/500m
Difficulty	Challenging
Walking time	6hr 30min
Maximum altitude	2905m
Refreshments	Consider visiting Friesenberg Hütte, beautifully located and just off the route.
Routefinding	Waymarking is generally very good apart from in the area around the glacier. The waymarks do exist but can be hard to spot particularly in early morning shadow. A GPS will be useful on this stretch.
Variants	In very bad weather, you should take buses via Mayrhofen round to the Olpererhütte or the Pfitscher Joch.

The highlight of Stage 11 is the Friesenbergscharte (2904m), the pass between the Hoher Riffler (3231m) and the Gefrorene-Wand-Sptizen (3288m). The ascent, which could well take place in the morning and in the shade, runs alongside a rapidly retreating glacier (this valley is not a good place for global warming sceptics), but it is the descent that really grabs the attention. Once again a head for heights is an essential pre-requisite on what is the Traumpfad's second stretch of sustained steel cable assisted walking. It's definitely a route best enjoyed in good weather.

As well as being a serious inconvenience it would be a shame to miss the Friesenbergscharte, It is a beautiful pass with great views. On my first trip over the pass the weather was poor, cloudy with fresh snow, but we made it – and so did all the Germans who were walking on a similar schedule.

BAD WEATHER OPTION VIA MAYRHOFEN

If the weather is really bad then the Friesenbergscharte should be bypassed but this involves some radical surgery as far as the route is concerned. You need to catch a bus (4104) from the bottom of the **Hintertux** ski lift down to Mayrhofen and from there another bus (4102) up to **Schlegeisspeicher** on the other side of the mountain. From Schelegiesspeicher pick up the 502 and climb up to the Olpererhütte – or, if short of time, follow the 524 along the valley to the Pfitscher Joch.

From the Tuxer Joch Haus walk along the dirt road heading east and zig-zagging down into the valley and towards the **Sommarberg Alm** ski station. After 700m leave the road (**1**) and turn right onto 326 and follow it across the valley (passing underneath a ski lift). Crossing a path (**2**) coming up from the Sommarberg Alm take the left hand fork and continue up to a dirt road. Follow the dirt road up to the Spannagelhaus (2530m) reached about 1hr 50min after leaving the Tuxer Joch Haus.

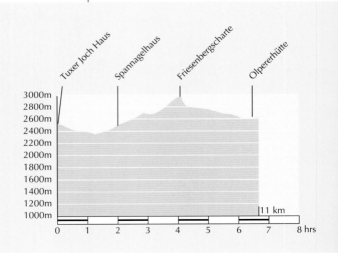

The Hintertux glacier and the Spannagelhaus boast the largest **cave system** in the central Alps. Guided tours, starting at 1000hrs, explore 500m of the 12.5km cave system and need to be booked a day in advance (**www.hintertuxergletscher.at** and choose 'Spannagelhöhle', tel 43 5287 87251).

From the Spannagelhaus leave the dirt road (which heads up to the Tuxer Ferner Haus) and join a path (the 526) heading southeast over a small bridge and into rocky terrain left by the retreating glacier. The path just about picks a route around the northern side (to the left) of the glacier. Finding the waymarks is a challenge, but they are there (a GPS is helpful). The climb gets steeper but it's relatively straightforward until the **Friesenbergscharte** (2904m) is reached.

The **view south** from a confined space between rocks at the top of the pass is breathtaking both for its scenery and, as is immediately apparent, for the

Descending from Freisenbergscharte

119

prospect of a challenging descent. A beautiful glacial lake lies in the foreground, the Friesenbergsee; a reservoir in the middle distance, the Schlegeisspeicher; with huge mountains beyond including the Großer Möseler (3480m) whose enormous glacier feeds into the reservoir.

From the pass follow a zig-zagging path steeply down the side of the mountain. The descent looks worse than it is: ropes and steel pins driven into the rock face add drama to the climb down.

Near the bottom (**3**) a sign points to the **Friesenberghaus** (2498m) (www.friesenberghaus.com tel 43 676 7497550) which sits in a beautiful location near the lake. If you are finishing the stage at the Olpererhütte there should be plenty of time to visit it and return on a different path to rejoin the main route.

From the turn-off to the Friesenberghaus to the Olpererhütte takes about 2hr. The path is good and gracefully contours its way south with just the occasional small stream to navigate. The route is now being shared with, among others, the famous Berliner Höhenweg so it is well maintained.

Arrival at the **Olpererhütte** (2389m) is announced by a little suspension bridge which, for those lucky enough to have travelled in Nepal, will bring back memories of the Himalaya.

From the outside the Olpererhütte looks like a large agricultural barn in need of a lick of paint. The inside presents a different story, spick and span with amazing views from the restaurant along the Schlegeisspeicher to the Großer Möseler. It would be a shame to arrive in the fog. Rebuilt in 2007, it's a modern hut and very comfortable (**www.olpererhuette.de**, tel 43 664 4176566).

STAGE 11B

Tuxer Joch Haus to the Geraerhütte

Start	Tuxer Joch Haus (2020m)
Distance	10km
Ascent/Descent	800m/700m
Difficulty	Moderate
Walking time	4hr 40min
Maximum altitude	2490m
Routefinding	The path has recently been rerouted on the approach to the Geraerhütte and this is not reflected on currently available maps.

The alternative way over the Tux Crest involves staying at the Geraerhütte, climbing over the ridge the next day via the Alpeiner Scharte and then rejoining the main route to south of the Olpererhütte. It's a lovely walk and an alternative to the less attractive traverse of the Hintertux ski resort but the Alpeiner Scharte is just as challenging as the Friesenbergscharte.

If the weather is perfect some walkers may find the walk from the Lizumer Hütte to Tuxer Joch Haus just a little short and consider continuing to the Geraerhütte. It's an epic challenge, involves includes another big 300m pass but the scenery in the late afternoon sun, could make it worth the effort.

From the Tuxer Joch Haus head south, climbing gently, along a dirt road following Route 527 and signs pointing to the Geraerhütte. After passing a reservoir full of water reserved for the snow cannon join a path. ▶ Now descending, continue along a lovely contour path along the eastern flank of a ridge to a pass, the **Kaserer Schartl** (2446m).

Cross the pass and continue around the southern end of a large valley (the Kaserer Winkl). Descending through myrtle bushes, laden with berries in September, the path gets steeper and eventually some 300m of altitude is lost.

An optional path climbs to the top of the Weiße Wand (2518m) rejoining the main route further on.

*Views from the
Kaserer Shartl*

The 527 has recently
been re-routed so
routes on maps tend
to be out of date.

After crossing streams at the bottom of the va ley continue along the 527 on a steep climb up to th **Kleegrubenscharte** (2490m). From this pass follow lovely path as it contours southeast. ◄

After crossing a little ridge (2476m) the **Olpere** (3476m) and its west-facing glacier become clear▶

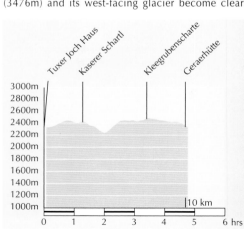

STAGE 11B – TUXER JOCH HAUS TO THE GERAERHÜTTE

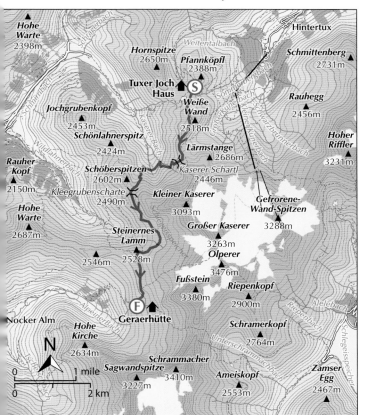

isible. Follow a new path, occasionally supported by
steel cables, as it swings around the base of the glacier
crossing streams in the process. As you join a grassy path
the Geraerhütte (2324m) should now be visible. The
route however has a sting in the tail. Before the hut is
reached a stream at the bottom of a gash in the glacial
debris has to be negotiated and if the weather is warm a
torrent of meltwater will make the crossing challenging.

The Geraerhütte (**www.geraerhuette.at**, tel 43 676 9610 303) is a lovely old hut that, away from the standard Traumpfad itinerary, should be quiet. Its occupants are attracted by the local climbs rather than long-distance hikes. It's an old-fashioned hut but with good facilities and excellent food.

STAGE 12A
Olpererhütte to Stein

Start	Olpererhütte (2390m)
Distance	13km
Ascent/Descent	400m/1310m
Difficulty	Moderate
Walking time	5hr 30min
Maximum altitude	2405m
Refreshments	The Pfitscherjoch Haus is a good place to stop for lunch although it will be busy on a sunny weekend.
Routefinding	Waymarking is excellent. The signs give this stage a black designation but there is nothing difficult to negotiate.

The 10km path between the Olpererhütte and Pfitscher Joch includes a beautifully engineered 'contour' path known as the Panorama Hohenweg and is a pure delight. Like most contour paths in the Alps the route is far from flat and, as it meanders its way into side valleys and around streams, it doesn't feel very direct either. However the constant views east into the highest mountains of the Zillertal are a great reward.

From the Olpererhütte follow the route south climbing gently as it swings around the head of a side valley. Cairns have been constructed on a grand scale and small towers of rock (reminiscent of chortens in Nepal) mark the path ahead. Descending into a side valley cross a wooden bridge over a stream and ignore the path (**1**) down the

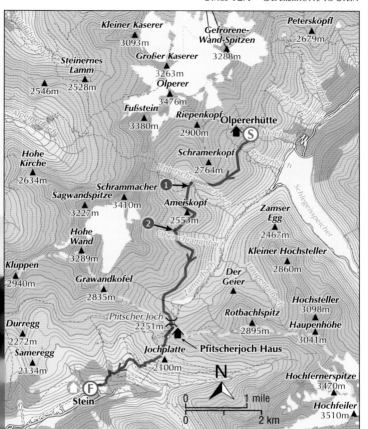

valley to the **Schlegeisspeicher** (535). Stage 12B joins the
path at this point. Continue south climbing up through
rocks and back onto the slab-lined path as it contours
once again across a saddle on the side of the valley.

This path, the **Panorama Hohenweg**, was built by
machine in 2006. Apparently 2600 slabs of rock

were positioned as part of its construction and the proud boast is that not one of them moves.

Follow the path swinging west into the next side valley and down to a stream (**2**). There is a pool just to the side and, although the water crashes through it, walkers (Germans of course) have been known to strip off and step into it for a very quick bath.

The temptation to cross the stream early should be avoided. It descends across sheer rock and the path has been carefully routed around it. In poor visibility and in the wet, crossing the stream could be hazardous.

Pfitscher Joch, the pass and the border with Italy, should now be clearly visible and is only an hour away.

From the stream follow the path east along the side valley and then south along the main valley. ◄ After an easy contouring walk the path descends into another side valley, across a bridge over a stream, for one final easy climb to make to the pass, the **Pfitscher Joch** (2251m), the border and the hut named after the pass.

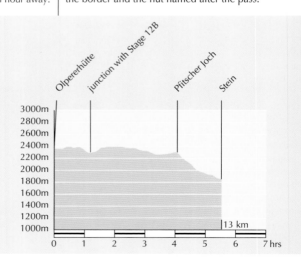

The Pfitscher Joch Haus (**www.pfitscherjochhaus.com**, tel 39 472 630119) is a private hut built originally in 1888. During the 1960s it was a focus for the political unrest in South Tyrol, was occupied by the military and was destroyed by a bomb in 1966 (an Italian officer was killed). It has recently been almost completely reconstructed and provides high quality accommodation designed to attract cyclists on the Transalp mountain bike route. The best room in the house is Room 8 – it has its own shower, luxury!

Although the '**Sud Tyrol**' is part of Italy it is very Germanic, part of Austria until the end of World War I and German-speaking. Subtle changes become immediately apparent, however. Yellow metal signs for the footpaths are replaced with wooden ones and everything has both a German and Italian name – the mountains, the huts and even the food (Wiener Schnitzel, the national dish of Austria is now also referred to as Bistecca alla Milanese). Although Italy is the third country on the Traumpfad the halfway point has still not been reached.

Over the Pfitscher Joch and into Italy

From the car park on the right hand side of Pfitscherjoch Haus follow Route 3 (now marked with wooden signs) down to Stein. The path drops east into a shallow valley and then heads south past some of border barracks. Heading steeply down the mountain side, initially across open grass land and then into pine forest, the route crosses the road meandering up to the pass four times as it swings west and drops into **Stein** (1565m).

> The Gasthof Stein (tel 39 472 630 130) is ancient with a lovely wood-panelled dining room. In terms of facilities it is a little basic but serves excellent food and is a magnet for Traumpfad walkers. If for whatever reason you need to leave the Traumpfad at this point a bus can be caught 30mins down the valley at Anger.

STAGE 12B
Geraerhütte to Stein

Start	Geraerhütte (2325m)
Distance	15km
Ascent/Descent	1210m/1960m
Difficulty	Challenging
Walking time	8hr 10min
Maximum altitude	2960m
Refreshments	The Pfitscherjoch Haus is a good place to stop for lunch although it will be busy on a sunny weekend.

From the Geraerhütte Stage 12B makes the short but dramatic traverse of the Tux Crest via the Alpeiner Scharte (2959m) before rejoining the standard itinerary in the valley below. The pass is just three metres lower than the highest point on the Traumpfad, which is reached on Stage 17 in the Dolomites and, with amazing views of the Zillertal Alps, is a more dramatic location.

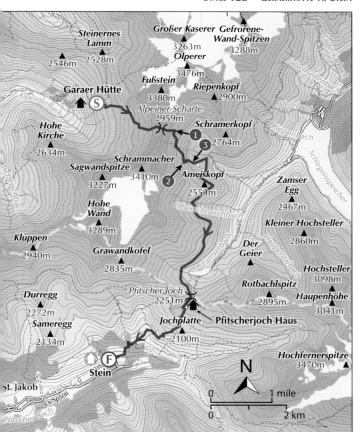

From the Geraerhütte head east along a path marked the [1]02 and signed to the Alpeiner Scharte. If you leave first thing in the morning the path will be in deep shade but [it]'s well marked and easy to follow.

As the path climbs the remains of a giant **World War II cable way** will be become increasingly apparent.

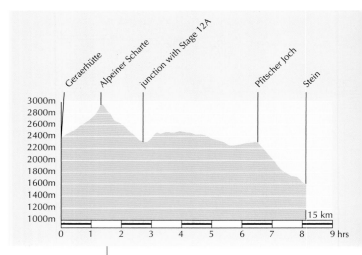

The remains are part of a mining complex where forced Ukrainian labour extracted molybdenum. Despite its size there is little documentation on the mine although it is recorded that in 1943 an avalanche killed 16 workers and injured a further 23.

Continue on the 502 to the **Alpeiner Scharte** (2959m), one of the most spectacular on the whole MV route. If you are lucky with the weather take time and enjoy amazing views across the valley to the Hochfeiler and its glacier.

The descent from the pass is hard and requires con centration. After about 40min the path swings north across a boulder field and from a platform (**1**) the views south down the valley open up. From here it's possible to see the Dolomites (a day earlier than on the standard route) and Marmolada with its distinct north-facing white glacier is clearly visible.

The path then switches direction and heads back across the slope, down to a stream and zig-zags its way down the southern side of the valley to a flume of glacia

scree. Turning north (**2**) and descending on the left hand side of the flume, a tricky traverse of a steep-sided gash in the gravel (**3**) is required before making a final easy descent down to two pretty little lakes beyond which the route joins the main route. Follow the route description in Stage 12A from here down to **Stein** (1565m).

The descent from Alpeiner Scharte

> The Gasthof Stein (tel 39 472 630 130) is ancient with a lovely wood-panelled dining room. In terms of facilities it is a little primitive but serves excellent food and is a magnet for Traumpfad walkers. If for whatever reason you need to leave the Traumpfad at this point a bus can be caught 30mins down the valley at Anger.

STAGE 13

Stein to Pfunders

Start	Gasthof Stein, Stein (1565m)
Distance	20km
Ascent/Descent	1200m/1550m
Difficulty	Challenging
Walking time	8hr 10min
Maximum altitude	1645m
Refreshments	Drinks are available at the Obere Engbergalm, about 5hr 30min from Stein, but food will need to be carried.
Routefinding	Navigation is easy and the route is generally well marked.

In Italy, with glimpses today of the Dolomites, it's tempting to think that the last lap has started. Such thoughts however would be distinctly premature – there is still lots of walking to do!

Stage 13 is a varied and dramatic. The highlight is definitely the climb up to the pass at the Gliderschartl and with amazing views on the way of the Hochfeiler, the highest mountain in the Zillertal Alps, and Höher Weißzint and the glacier that flows down it.

Once the pass has been crossed it's downhill all the way. The stretch from Dun to Pfunders, which looks a little boring on the map, is surprisingly pleasant and follows an old engineered trail that may have had a military past.

STARTING FROM THE PFITSCHERJOCH HAUS

If you stayed at Pfitscher Joch rather than Stein follow Route 3 down the hill. After descending for 20min or so down a steep hill the route joins a road, turn right and continues towards to Stein. Leave the road after a few metres joining a path that cuts out a switchback and rejoins the road below. Instead of going to Stein turn left along a road and head down to a small car park. Here the route joins the main route from Stein.

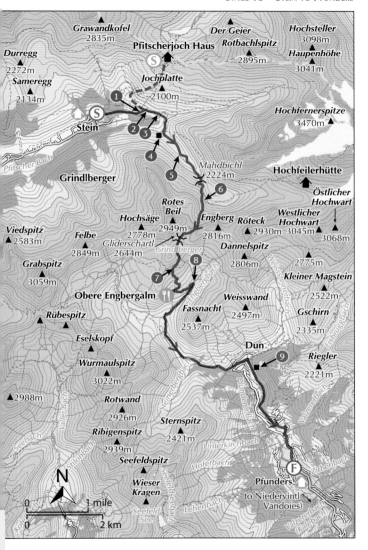

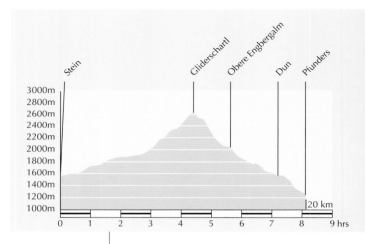

Head east along the road from the Gasthof for 1.2km. As the road swings west around a switchback join a path (**1**) and continue east, climbing steadily until the road is rejoined (**2**) after 300m. Follow the road to car park (**3**), a starting point for hikers and climbers embarking on a huge array of local walks and climbs, including a walk to the top of the Hochfeiler.

The Hochfeiler from just beyond the Pfitscher Joch

From the car park follow the path marked 1 and 8 steeply down through trees towards the stream. ▸ Once the stream is crossed the path climbs quickly over a shoulder to some small farm buildings and a fork in the path (**4**). Leave Route 1 to continue its journey up to the Hochfeilerhütte and head southeast (along Route 8) into the stunning Gliderbach valley.

Initially the walking is easy. The path stays close to the left hand side of the stream and the only challenges are electric cattle fences. After crossing a bridge (**5**) and crossing streams running down the western side of the valley the path starts its climb to the **Mahdbichl** (2224m), a saddle on the valley side.

> The **views back down the valley** become ever more distracting with the Pfitscherjoch Haus now clearly visible but these are quickly eclipsed as the world of the Hochfeiler (3510m) and Höher Weißzint (3371m) emerge to the east. It's a dramatic scene with enormous white peaks, well illuminated if you're lucky, emerging from huge but retreating glaciers below in what looks like a desolate grey valley.

Now the real work begins. After passing a junction (**6**) with a path heading east and down into the valley, the route climbs steeply but steadily up to the **Gliderschartl** (2644m).

> The views are great but, unless the weather is good, the **pass** is not a place to linger. It can be cold with patches of snow persisting most of the year. Although there is little in the way of grass you can expect to see gentians and harebells.

Continue south from the pass to the little glacial lake, the **Grindlberger** (2485m), where hardy swimmers might be tempted to take a dip. Just beyond the lake the route starts its descent into particularly beautiful green alpine valley, the Engbergalm, but before going too far down

Landslips have necessitated some recent path rerouting and the construction of a new footbridge.

the path have a look south to the horizon where, if the weather is good, the distinct profile of the Dolomites should be visible. Head directly south down the grassy side of the valley, crossing a junction (**7**) with the Pfunderer Höhenweg, and continue for about 50mins, to the **Obere Engbergalm** (2123m) where cold drinks can be purchased.

Follow the farm access track west then east as it switchbacks its way down to a stream (shortcuts can be taken). Crossing the stream (**8**) join a concrete road heading west, south and then east down the valley and around a ridge of mountains. After about an hour's easy walking from the Obere Engbergalm, tracking a ferocious stream and entering a wooded valley, the route arrives at the scattered community of **Dun** (1530m).

The concrete road has now joined a tarmac road. Follow the tarmac road east for about 200m, staying with it as crosses a stream and swings southeast past some houses and farm buildings (**9**). Where the tarmac ends, follow Route 13 along a beautiful old engineered road, now abandoned, as it traverses its way along the side of the valley. The new road is below. After 2km of shady walking the path emerges into alpine meadows and scattered hillside farmsteads. Ahead and below is the village of **Pfunders** (1150m). After joining a metalled access road the route turns right and heads down to the main road.

The friendly Gasthof Brugger (**www.gasthof-brugger. com**, tel 39 0472 549 155) is located about 600m down the road near the cashpoint.

3 PFUNDERS TO ALLEGHE

In the Val Setus (Stage 17)

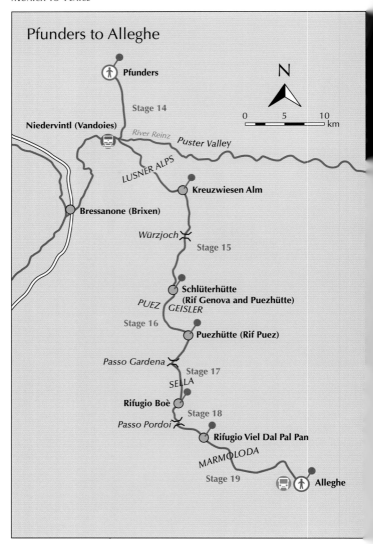

Albergo Savoia with a Sella backcloth (Stage 18)

Section 3 is all about the Dolomites, one of the world's most popular walking destinations.

The Dolomites are different. From a distance the profile of countless steeples and pinnacles is instantly recognisable and sets them apart from everything else in the Alps. Close up it's the special colours that catch the eye. The Sella Massif one of the best places to experience a sunset as you watch its magnesium limestone turn a magical rusty gold. Unesco has designated the Dolomites a World Heritage Landscape saying that it 'features some of the most beautiful mountain landscapes anywhere, with vertical walls, sheer cliffs and a high density of narrow, deep and long valleys' and who are we to argue?

From Pfunders, or Niedervintl (Vandoies) if only this section is being walked, it takes a day and a half to get to the Dolomites. The Puster valley has to be crossed and the gentle Lüsner Alps traversed before reaching a north Dolomite outlier Peitlerköfel (2875m) just north of the Schlüterhütte on your second night. The scenery now transforms and for the next four days the route plunges into the heart of the Dolomites visiting three of its most important sub-divisions, the Puéz Geisler, Sella and Marmolada groups.

From a distance some of the paths look steep and intimidating but their bark is worse than their bite. A number of stretches involve fixed steel cables and ropes but by this point in the route these should be something to be relished rather than feared. The trails are well used and clearly marked and the route from Stage 17 to Stage 19 follows the same route as the famous Alta Via 2, one of Italy's most popular trails.

ACCESS AND ACCOMMODATION

Alleghe, at the end of this stretch, is not on a railway line but is well connected by bus to Belluno. It takes two to three hours to get from Belluno to Venice by train.

The Dolomites can be crowded in August, particularly at midday on the Sella when the flow of day trippers deposited by a huge cable car onto the plateau reaches its peak. The number of people staying high overnight is limited by the capacity of the huts but in August they will be busy. You need to book ahead especially for exquisitely positioned huts like the Schlüterhütte. Hotels on the famous Dolomite passes – Grodner Joch (Passo Gardena) and Pordoi Joch (Passo Pordoi) – provide an alternative to the huts and for some walkers it may be worth trading in a perfect sunset for a good night's sleep.

KEY INFORMATION

Distance	103km
Total ascent	5510m
Total descent	5720m
Alternative schedule	The six stages in this section correspond to the 'German schedule' and apart from the last one all finish at a mountain hut. If you have walked all the way from Munich you will now be fit and the days will feel easier. If you want to avoid the mountain huts, a five-day schedule staying in hotels is feasible. This involves finishing Stage 16 at Würzjoch (6hr 20min), Stage 17 at Passo Gardena (9hr 30min), Stage 18 at Passo Pordoi (6hr 20min) and Stage 19 at Alleghe (7hr 15min). Stage 17 is a long but truly epic walk and avoids the Puezhütte (Rifugio Puez), which can be grim if crowded. A further alternative, useful if the Schlüterhütte is full, is to stay at the small, fairly basic hut at Medalges Alm, 45 mins further along the trail. From Medalges Alm it's 7hr 10min to the hotel at Pordoi Joch (again avoiding the Puezhütte).

STAGE 14

Pfunders to Kreuzwiesen Alm

Start	Gasthof Brugger, Pfunders (1155m)
Distance	24km
Ascent/Descent	1500m/800m
Difficulty	Moderate
Walking time	8hr
Maximum altitude	1925m
Refreshments	Niedervintl (Vandoies), whether reached by foot or on the bus, has a supermarket and is a good place to 'stock up'. The Roner Hütte, which is about 1hr 40min from the end of walk does hot food if required.
Variant	You could take an early morning bus to shorten the walk.

Stage 14 provides a relaxing and easy interlude between the tough alpine walking through Tux and Zillertal Alps and the drama that waits in the Dolomites.

It is a long day but doesn't have to be. Most German walkers catch the bus first thing to shorten it. This involves either staying on the bus for the first four kilometres and getting off at the bridge marked 2 on the map, or going all the way to Niedervintl. This reduces walking time by either 1hr or 3hr if you go all the way to Niedervintl.

The walking is straightforward. The first part completes yesterday's walk down the Pfunders Valley to Niedervintl. At Niedervintl, where the River Pfunder (Pfunderer Bach) meets the larger River Eisack, the route crosses the Puster Valley, an important transport corridor, and then embarks on a steady climb through trees on its southern side to Kreuzwiesen Alm.

From the Gasthof Brugger follow the road south for 800m (**1**). Turn left off the main road, join an access road (parallel but above the main road) and head southeast past some farm buildings. Continue south for 1.4km (the access road turns into a path and then a road again) before descending to the main road. Follow the main road south for another 1.9km to a bridge (**2**). ▶

If you've caught the bus and want to get off before going down to Niedervintl, ask the driver to drop you off here.

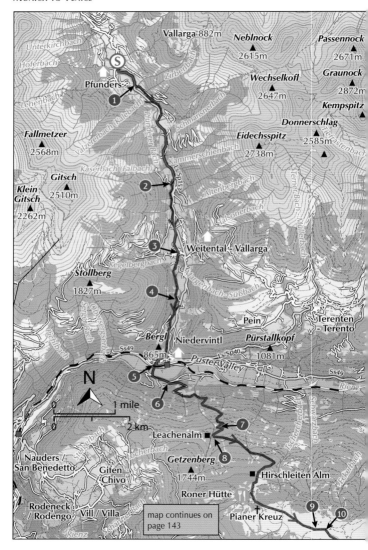

map continues on
page 143

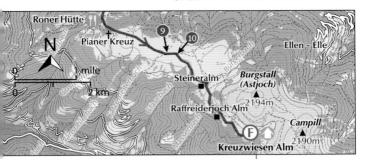

Cross the bridge over the river and after about 100m, turn left onto a path and head south following signs to **Vallarga**. Follow a path through trees for 1km to a metalled road and continue on it for another kilometre into the centre of the village (882m).

There is accommodation at Vallarga at the Haus Gitschberg (**www.haus-gitschberg.com**, tel 39 472 548057), a ski hotel offering great value in the summer.

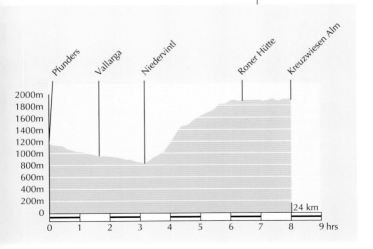

As the main road swings east and down the hill, turn right (**3**) and head south along a route with signs marked '4.2km from Vallarga' join an access road (**4**) and continue south down to the river.

Leave the road just before the bridge, stay on the right hand side of the river and follow a path for 800m into **Niedervintl** (760m). Finally crossing the river the route emerges into the centre of the town near a bank and information boards.

There is surprisingly little accommodation in Niedervintl itself and the best option is the Lodenwirt (**www.lodenwirt.com**, tel 39 472 867000) just to the east of the town. The supermarket is on the main road opposite the information boards.

Turn right at the junction into the centre of the town and the follow the main road west and down the hill towards the River Reinz. Follow Route 14 signs to the Roner Hütte, walking through an underpass beneath the motorway (**5**) and continuing south across a bridge over the river. Turn left on the other side of the bridge

The wooden barn at Leachenalm

nd continue east along a road parallel with the river for 00m. Turn right (**6**) and join a forest road (initially met-led and still marked Route 14) as it switchbacks its way o the side of the valley. After walking for about 25min ollow a path up the mountainside along path (Route 14). rossing forest roads and taking a more indirect route e path continues south up the mountainside through ees for another 50min before finally emerging onto a orest road and a junction (**7**) with Route 14A (signs to bervintl). Turn right and head west northwest into a eadow known as **Leachenalm** (1434m).

Cross to the southwest side of the Leachenalm, turn ast and follow a forest road past an old wooden barn. the north, above the line of the trees is a view over e Puster Valley and up the Pfunders Valley. Immediately ter the barn turn right at a fork (**8**) and head south back to trees. After 50m turn right again and head southwest r 300m, still following Route 14. The route then turns ft, heads southeast and climbs gently along a forest ad for 1.8km. ▶

This is an area where forestry work may affect the route.

Swing southwest and south and after 600m emerge ar wooden buildings into meadows known as the **irschleiten Alm** (1810m). Continue south along the estern side of the meadow and the boundary with the rest, and the **Roner Hütte** (1832m) should soon come to view.

The Roner Hütte (**www.ronerhuette.it**, tel 39 472 546016) is a private hut providing food and accommodation. It's in the middle of an accessible and popular walking area and can be busy.

From the junction west of the Roner Hütte follow ute 2 (now helpfully marked München Venedig) south-st along a path and then a gravel road reaching the tiny ooden chapel, the **Pianer Kreuz** after 15mins.

About 200m beyond the chapel is the **Leier Alm** with a helpful panoramic board naming the surrounding mountains. The most striking and

significant is the Peitlerköfel, a northern outlier of
the Dolomites and tomorrow's target.

Continue east-southeast across the open Lüsner Al
for 1.2km, reaching a junction (**9**) with Route 3. Ignore tl
right hand turn and continue east for another 300m, tur
ing right (**10**) onto Route 2A signed to Kreuzwiesen. Leav
the gravel track and head southeast along a path acro
fields. After a kilometre the path crosses a small gully, th
a dirt road and climbs across a field and past farm buil
ings (**Steineralm** 1908m). Continue south then southea
through several cattle fences and past what looks like
old hut, the **Raffreiderjoch Alm**, to a dirt road. Follow tl
east for about 500m to the **Kreuzwiesen Alm** (1925m).

The Kreuzwiesen Alm (**www.kreuzwiesenalm.com**,
tel 39 472 413 714) is a private hut with good food (it
makes its own cheese) and a range of different types of
room, including a very large dormitory unfortunately
positioned above the cowshed. When I stayed there
the smell was very agricultural although I'm not sure
whether the cows can really be held responsible.

STAGE 15
*Kreuzwiesen Alm to the Schlüterhütte
(Rifugio Genova)*

Start	Kreuzwiesen Alm (1925m)
Distance	22km
Ascent/Descent	1370m/990m
Difficulty	Moderate
Walking time	8hr 30min
Maximum altitude	2360m
Refreshments	The Maurerberghütte, recently restored, serves good food and is an ideal place to fuel up before the last gruelling section of the day.

Stage 15 is a walk of two halves, the first completing the gentle journey across the Lüsner Alm and the second providing the first taste of the Dolomites.

The distinct shape and colour of the Peitlerköfel has already served as a taste of what's ahead but it's only once the Peitlerscharte is crossed that classic Dolomite walking really starts. The walk from the pass up to the perfectly located Schlüterhütte (Rifugio Genova) is stunning and makes use of a beautiful high-level contour walk with amazing views east across the Val Badia into Sasso Santa Croce. It's hard to believe that this quality of walking is sustained all the way to the Marmolada, not reached for another 3½ days.

This is a long day and the hard work is towards the end. A lot of height is lost crossing the valley in front of the Würzjoch and the Peitlerscharte (Forcella di Putia) requires you to climb another 300m at the end of the day.

Head east from the Kreuzwiesen Alm past the dormitory with the cowshed underneath along a farm road following Route 2A. Stay on the farm road for 600m but as it swings south and down, leave it (**1**) to join a path crossing a field. Continue east-northeast for 500m following signs to Jacob Stöckl. At a junction (**2**) join Route 10 and follow it south across the valley, over a gate and onto a road. From here there are two ways to Jacob Stöckl. Take

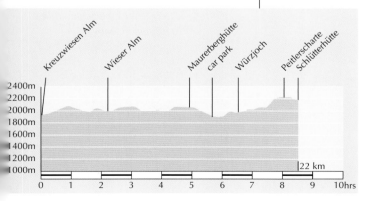

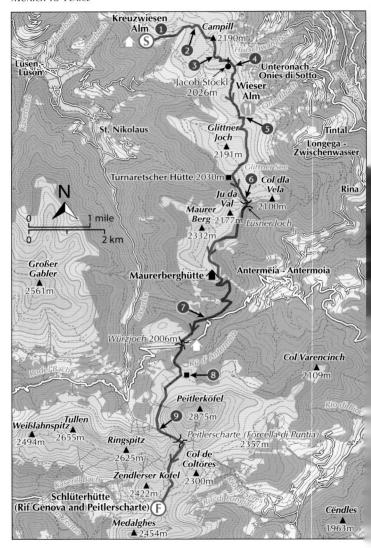

The Glittner See

the route that climbs gently up **Campill** (2190m) 5min to he east. ▸

From the summit head south (crossing a fence) and after 600m rejoin Route 10 (**3**). Head southeast and turn right at a junction (**4**) with Route 2. **Jacob Stöckl** (2026m), a small wooden chapel with a bench, is reached after a few metres. Continue south along Route 10 for 1.4km to the **Wieser Alm** (2015m) where refreshments may be available in season.

Head east past the Wieser Alm and then turn south (**5**), still on Route 10, following signs to the Turnaretscher Hütte. After 1.2km and a gentle climb the route arrives at the **Glittner See**, a small slightly surreal upland lake on which a wooden boat has been deposited. From the Glittner See the route heads southwest down a path to the **Turnaretscher Hütte** (2030m) (closed in August 2014).

Continue past the hut and after 700m (10min) turn right at a junction (**6**), down a narrow path through trees and follow a sign marked 1A to the Lüsner Joch. **Lüsner Joch**, a pass on the route between Brixen and Untermoi is reached after 100m. Here two signs, the 1

From a handily placed bench at the top the views north into the Zillertal Alps are excellent.

and the 1A point to the Maurerberghütte. 1A climbs ove
the Maurer Berg (2332m) so take Route 1. The route fo
lows a forest road that turns into a path after a kilometre
Climbing slightly the path contours around side of th
valley, passing through old pine trees and reaching th
Maurerberghütte (2157m) about 50min after the Lüsne
Joch.

> The Maurerberghütte (**www.maurerberg.com**, tel 39
> 474 520059) is a private hut that has recently been
> rebuilt and, as well as delicious food, also provides
> accommodation. Its sun terrace is a delightful place
> to relax and enjoy the views of the north face of
> Peitlerköfel across the valley.

Leave the hut and continue on Route 1. Initially th
route switchbacks its way down the mountainside on
path but then joins a gravel road and follows it down t
the main road and a car park (**7**) (1870m). Cross the ca
park and follow the path southwest up a steep hillsid
through trees to the **Würzjoch** (2006m).

> Towering above the Würzjoch is the mighty
> **Peitlerköfel**, demonstrating conclusively to anyone
> with any doubts that the Dolomites start here. Note
> that place names are now sometimes in three lan-
> guages, German, Italian and Ladin.

> Würzjoch has a very comfortable good quality hotel
> (**www.wuerzjoch.com**, tel 39 0474 52 00 66) and if
> last night was spent above the cows at Kreuzwiesen
> Alm this could be good place to stop.

Cross the road past information boards and follov
Route 8A south along a dirt road towards the north fac
of Peitlerköfel. After a kilometre the dirt road ends at
hut, the Munt de Fornela. Turn right onto a path (**8**) an
follow it west then southwest around the mountain an
into a valley. Continue south along an easy stony pat
(the route has now entered the Puez Geisler Natur

ark) for about 30min to a junction (**9**) with paths arriv-
ng from the west. Swing east around the mountain along
n increasingly narrow valley (now marked Route 4) and
limb steeply for 40min up to the pass, the **Peitlerscharte**
r Forcella di Putia (2357m). ▶

The last part of the
climb is sheltered and
early in the season
could have snow.

On the climb up the pass the Traumpfad joins the
Alta Via 2 and stays on it for three days before
finally leaving it at Malga Ciapela. The waymarks, a
red triangle encasing the figure two, are easy to spot
but, in any event, providing the weather is good,
navigation is very straightforward.

At the pass routes shoot off in various directions
cluding one which heads north and up a cable-assisted
ute to the top of the **Peitlerkofel**. Our route on the other
and heads south along a stunning contour path crossing
eadows full of cattle. From the pass it's just 30min to
e **Schlüterhütte** or Rifugio Genova (2301m).

The Schlüterhütte (**www.schlueterhuette.com**, tel 39
0472 670072) is one best huts on the whole Traumpfad.
Its location, on the western edge of the Dolomites and
nestled between 2500m peaks to north and south, is
exceptional. Although extensively modernised it still
retains some of the original timber construction which
dates back to 1898. It's also a lively place with a reputation for music and even dancing although participa-
tion is not compulsory.

STAGE 16
Schlüterhütte to the Puezhütte

Start	Schlüterhütte (Rifugio Genova) (2300m)
Distance	11km
Ascent/Descent	740m/560m
Difficulty	Challenging
Walking time	5hr
Maximum altitude	2720m
Refreshments	Apart from an early morning break at the Medalgesalm there is nowhere to stop for refreshments. If you need something organise a picnic lunch at the Schlüterhütte. Navigation is easy and the way marking excellent.
Variants	Forcella Roa and Forcella Nives can be avoided, in case of a fear of heights or in bad weather (see below).

Stage 16 is pure unadulterated Dolomite walking at its very best. If the weather is half decent it's an absolute treat with views that are truly spectacular.

There are two stretches that from a distance look intimidating but are not nearly as bad on closer inspection. The first pass, the Forcella Roa, is approached on a switchbacking path up a steep open bank of scree. It looks tough and is visible from a long way out but the path is never less than a metre wide. The second pass is the Forcella Nives climbed shortly after the Forcella Roa and approached along a path which first traverses steep scree. The hundred metres of ascent to the Forcella Nives looks vertical and well beyond the competency of the 'average walker', but the cable-assisted climb up a 'chimney' is more straightforward than it looks and the views from the top are excellent so try not be put off.

Bad weather alternative
If the weather is bad both passes could be avoided following the Adolf Munkel Weg southwest from t Schlüterhütte. This alternative (Route 35) heads do the valley until it hits Route 6 and climbs southeast ov

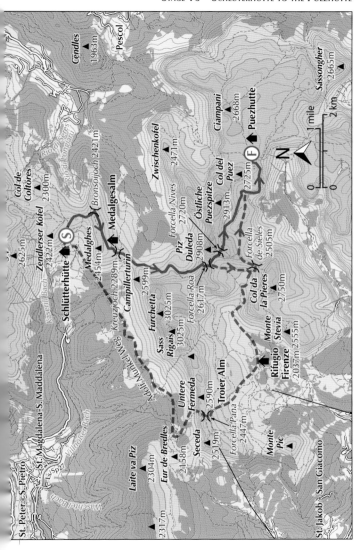

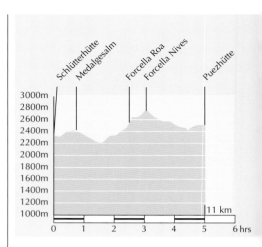

the **Forcella Pana** (2447m). From the pass it takes Rou
1 down to the **Troier Alm** (2271m) and then continu
to the **Rifugio Firenze** (2037m) and then up to Forcel
de Sieles to the variant described below for avoiding th
Forcella Nives. This option takes an additional 2hr an
still involves some exposed walking along a ridge.

For the main route head southeast from the Schlüterhüt
(Rifugio Genova) and south up to the **Bronsoijoc**
(2421m).

> The **views from the pass** are excellent. Immediately
> to the north is Peiterköfel and behind it, to the
> east, the Zillertal Alps. Towards the northeast is
> Kreuzkofel with Cunturines to the east. South is
> the Geisler Púez group. Our pass, the Forcella Roa
> which sits between the Púez Group to the southeast
> and the Geisler group to the southwest, should be
> clearly visible.

From the Bronsoijoch follow a well-defined trail ru
ning through an alpine meadow west, southwest dov

The approach to Forcella Roa

o the **Medalgesalm** (2293m) (the alternative overnight top to the Schlüterhütte (www.medalges.com, tel 39 347 i049169) and the pass at **Kreuzjoch** (2289m).

The meadow here is particularly rich in **flowers** including, if you're lucky, edelweiss. Immediately ahead the summits of the Geisler group Sas Rigais (3025m) and Furchetta (3025m) should be visible.

Without crossing the pass, continue south past the reuzjoch along a path running along the eastern flank f the Geisler group. After 40min it starts to climb and witchback its way up the scree. The path is steep and xposed but wide and safe. It takes 25 to 30min of slow nd steady plodding to climb 200m to the top of the orcella Roa (2617m), a good place to stop and steady our nerves for the next challenge.

voiding Forcella Nives

orcella Nives can be avoided by descending from the orcella Roa along Route 3. After 200m take a left hand rn and head south and across the head of the valley to join Route 2. Turn left and follow the path as it climbs steeply to the **Forcella de Sieles** (2505m).

Main route continues

◀ To get to the **Forcella Nives** (2720m) head southeast across a steep bank of scree following Route 3A. This is turns out to be the most intimidating part and the climb up the cliff face, helped by steel cables, is straightforward.

Once on top the views from **Forcella Nives** are breathtaking. To the southwest, highlighted with white glaciers, are the Adamello-Presanella Alps, whose summits are over 3500m. Immediately to the south is the huge plateau of the Sella group, crossed tomorrow, and to the southeast the distinctively shape Civetta Dolomites crossed in four days' time. Directly east, and perhaps the highlight of the whole panorama is Mont Pelmo (3168m), which stands alone and is arguably the most beautiful mountain in all the Dolomites. To the north and easily accessed (30mins) along a gentle rising

Climbing the Forcella Nives

path across arid grey limestone is the Piz Duleda (2908m).

The rest of the walk is easy, and, after the challenge of crossing two intimidating passes, is a thing to be savoured. Continue east southeast along a gently descending path (still Route 3A) into the Puezalm. After 30min the route joins the variant descending from the Forcella de Sieles. The route swings south and east again before arriving at the **Puezhütte** or Rifugio Puez (2475m) 30min later.

The Puezhütte (**www.rifugiopuez.it**, tel 39 0471 795 365) is beautifully located with a south-facing sun terrace, and a great spot for an afternoon beer and strudel. It's very remote and supplies are flown in by helicopter. It's also very cramped and the dormitory is small, under the eaves without enough room for rucksacks. A full Puezhütte dormitory is not to everyone's taste. The Grödner Joch (Passo Gardena) is 2hr to 2hr 30min away and makes an excellent late afternoon extension to the day. If sleep is a priority it's the best option.

STAGE 17

Puezhütte (Rifugio Puez) to Rifugio Boè

Start	Puezhütte (Rifugio Puez) (2475m)
Distance	14km
Ascent/Descent	1270m/860m
Difficulty	Challenging
Walking time	6hr 50min
Maximum altitude	2960m
Refreshments	There are places to eat at Grodner Joch (Passo Gardena) and Rifugio Pisciadù.
Routefinding	Navigation and waymarking is excellent.
Variant	Extend this stage by climbing Piz Boè from Rifugio Boè along Route 638 to stay at Refugio Capanna Fassa (an additional 50min and 300m climb).

Stage 17 finishes the journey across the Geisler Púez and after crossing the Grodner Joch, heads into the heart of the Sella. It's another amazing day in the Dolomites and climbs to the highest point on the Traumpfad.

The day involves 1270m of ascent and more work with cables. But the climbs are not as exposed or as intimidating as those on Stage 16 and should be approached with confidence.

Depending on the weather, time of year and time of day the crowds might come as surprise. The Sella is popular and very accessible, particularly from the south, with cable cars taking huge numbers to the top. The Grodner Joch, to the north and Passo Pordo to the south are also a huge draw for both cyclists and motorcyclists so expect to see a lot of lycra and leather at each of the passes.

Staying at the Rifugio Capanna Fassa is worth considering either as detour from the main route, or as an alternative to the Rifugio Boè. Sitting on the highest point in the Sella Group (3152m) the views are by reputation among the best in the Dolomites and include the Marmolada, Pelmo and Civetta. Timing is particularly important. Midday and early afternoon in good weather in August means huge crowds. By late afternoon the crowds will have gone and the spectacular sunsets and sunrises can be enjoyed in relative peace.

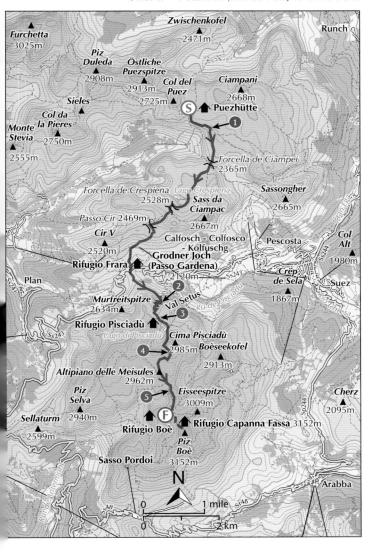

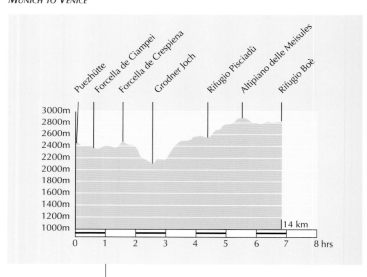

From the Puezhütte (Rifugio Puez) head east southeast along Route 2 to the Grodner Joch. After 15min turn south at a junction (**1**) with Route 5 and continue along Route 2. The route arcs around the valley and the Puezalm. After another 20min the path reaches a pass, the **Forcella de Ciampei** (2365m), with views down the valley to the Civetta. Without descending, continue south and then ignoring the Route 2A turnoff swing southwest. ◀

It's a lovely easy path with great views of the Odle needles towards the northwest in the Geisler Group.

Continue southwest still following Route 2 along a grassy path. Immediately below and to the northwest is the **Lago Crespiena**, an inviting spot but perhaps too early to stop for lunch. The path then starts a 100m switchback climb to the **Forcella de Crespiena** (2528m) which is topped with a fence and a cross.

From the pass head west directly towards the distinctive profile of the beautiful Sassolungo (3181m) and follow a well-defined path along the side of a classic limestone valley. After 30min you reach the **Passo Cir** (2469m) and the path climbs out of the valley into a weird landscape of eroded mini-summits and spires (known as

Danter les Pizes). After 30min, and a steep descent, the path emerges into a world of chairlifts, Jimmy's Hut and, depending on the time of day, road traffic at the **Grodner Joch** or Passo Gardena (2120m).

View from the Forcella de Crespiena

> There are two hotels on the pass itself both of which are good value – the Rifugio Frara (the sign on the building is Refugio Alpino) (**www.rifugiofrara.it**, tel 39 0471 795225) and the Hotel Cir (**www.hotelcir.com**, tel 39 0471 795127).

Rejoin the path from the car park on the western side of the Rifugio Frara (now Route 666) and follow it southeast underneath the cliffs of the Sella massif. After 30min the path turns south (**2**) and climbs into a deep dark gash in the side of the Sella, the **Val Setus** (north facing and deep it gets very little sun and snow lingers here for most of the year). Continuing up the path gets steeper, first crossing open scree and then climbing, with the assistance of cables, an almost vertical rock face. If

Rifugio Pisciadù

the weather is good the darkness of the gorge will contrast sharply with brightness of the valley beyond. From the terrace at the top of the pass (2606m) (**3**) the views north into the Geisler Púez group are excellent, a perfect place to take a photograph.

Continue southeast through a boulder field to the **Rifugio Pisciadù** (2587m).

Yet another beautifully-located hut, the Rifugio Pisciadù (tel 39 471 836292) sits just above a small lake, the Lago di Pisciadù, and features a tempting sun terrace. This area is popular for its via ferratas so if a stop is made expect to share it with climbers wearing harnesses and helmets. Above the hut, to the southeast, is the Cima Pisciadù (2985m) and the sheer yellow flank of its western side.

Still following Route 666 head south past the lake climb and gently along a path cutting across scree to the west of **Cima Pisciadù**. As the path heads east into the

Val de Tita it gets steeper and again fixed cables are positioned to help the climb. Above the cable in a shallow gully expect to find snow. About 10min after the cables the route turns right and continues south at a junction (**4**) with another route heading up the Cima Pisciadù. Swing southwest and start an easy climb which levels out onto a plateau, the **Altipiano delle Meisules**. ▶

At 2962m this is the highest point on the Traumpfad.

Descend south-southeast to the head of the Val di Mesdi (**5**) among stunning rock formations and sheer cliffs. Ahead is **Piz Boè** on top of which sits some ugly communication equipment. In the day-time it could be packed with day-trippers disgorged from the huge cable car which runs up to the nearby **Sasso Pordoi**. Beneath that the **Rifugio Boè** (2873m) should be visible.

The Rifugio Boè (**www.rifugioboe.it**, tel 39 0471 847303), with its distinct blue and white shutters, is an Italian Alpine Club Hut. It serves good food but in other respects is a little basic – there is no shower. Close by and on top of the Piz Boè itself is the Rifugio Capanna Fassa. This is a 'cosy' but very special place to stay and, once the cable car has stopped, serenely quiet. At 3152m, this is the highest place that you can sleep (indoors!) on the Traumpfad (**www.rifugio capannapizfassa.com**, tel 39 3385 4736 24).

STAGE 18

Rifugio Boè to Rifugio Viel dal Pan

Start	Rifugio Boè (2875m)
Distance	8km
Ascent/Descent	400m/840m
Difficulty	Challenging
Walking time	4hr
Maximum altitude	2875m
Refreshments	There are plenty of places to stop for refreshments.
Routefinding	Navigation continues to be straightforward helped by excellent waymarking.
Variant	Extend this stage by climbing Piz Boè along Route 638 (an additional 50min and 300m climb) before you set off.

Stage 18 completes the traverse of the Sella Group, crosses another pass at the Passo Pordoi and embarks on a particularly enjoyable stretch of walking along a grassy ridge facing the northern side of the Marmolada, 'the Queen of the Dolomites'. It is relatively short and there are lots of accommodation options between Rifugio Boè and Alleghe that make for easy extensions to the day. Alternatively there is time before the crowds arrive to make it up to the Piz Boè, a detour that adds 50min to the walk.

The day's main challenge is a very steep descent across scree from the Rifugio Forcella Pordoi, a descent that could be avoided by taking cable down from the Sasso Pordoi.

Head south from the Rifugio Boè along Route 627 going directly to Rifugio Forcella Pordoi or on Route 6_ if going there via Piz Boè. After the path back down fro Piz Boè rejoins the main route, there is a short stret of cable-assisted walking and then the route swin west and down to the pass, the **Forcella Pordoi**, and h named after it (reached after about 50min).

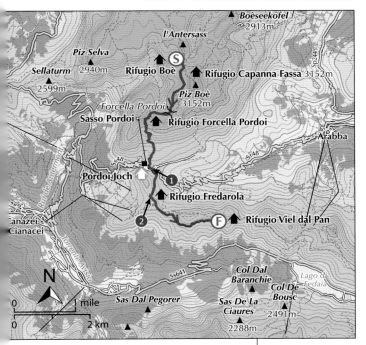

The Rifugio Forcella Pordoi (2850m) (tel 39 368 355
7505), clearly visible from the Rifugio Boè, is located
on the edge of the Sella Massif and immediately underneath the Sasso Pordoi. It's privately run and a very
friendly place, perfect for cup of coffee, almost essential fortification for the next challenge of the day.

After passing through an area where there will prob-
ly be patches of snow, follow a steep path switchback-
ʒ its way down a bank of scree. The descent to **Pordoi**
ᴄh or Passo Pordoi (2239m) is 600m and it's definitely
ssible for those with nerves of steel, flexible knees and
e necessary technique, to run down. Most people make
nore leisurely 60 to 90min descent.

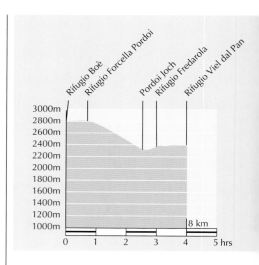

Pordoi Joch, the main access point to the Sella, is very lively. As well as coaches dropping off day-trippers it's a major destination for cyclists and motorcyclists (and regularly part of the Giro d'Italia). The Hotel Savoia (**www.savoiahotel.net**, tel 39 (462 601717) is particularly comfortable – good value, excellent food and with great views of the Sella from the dining room. If you stay here you can definitely make it to Alleghe next day.

Rejoin the route by turning off the road between th Casa Alpina and the Hotel Savoia (**1**) following Route 6C and AV2 heading southeast. As the path swings aroun the Sas Bece it passes a small chapel. Walk south fc 500m along a gently climbing path to a junction (**2** Turn left and head southeast underneath a chairlift, to th east of the Rifugio Sass Beccei, and across to the **Rifug Fredarola** (2394m) (www.fredarola.it, tel 39 462 60207 (about 400m from the junction).

From the rifugio follow a well-defined path ea along the grassy southern flank of ridge all the way 1 Rifugio Viel dal Pan (2436m) reached 30min later.

The path, which provides amazing views of the glacier on the north face of the Marmolada, is called the **Viel del Pan** (the 'Way of Bread' because it was originally used by flour merchants) and is an old mule path. (In German it's named the Bindelweg after Dr Karl Bindel, one of the original DAV pioneers.)

Approaching Marmolada on the Viel del Pan

THE MARMOLADA

The ridge you follow to the refuge is volcanic and the distinct black gritty rock is the remainder of an ancient lava flow and part of the Padon chain (Mt Padon 2510m, is further east) which flanks the north and eastern side of the Marmolada. These volcanic elements make the Marmolada geologically distinct and even the limestone, grey and without the golden yellow tinges of the Sella, is different. Although clearly a single 'massif', the Marmolada is just one mountain but includes a number of summits, many over 3000m. The two highest points, Punta Penia (3343m) and Punta Rocca (3309), are the highest in the Dolomites.

The Punta Penia was first climbed in 1864 by Paul Grohmann but it was a pioneering English woman climber, Beatrice Tomasson, who first summited via the south face in 1901.

167

The most distinctive feature of the Marmolada, particularly from the north, is the glacier which can be seen from great distances and is the last surviving glacier in the Dolomites. The Marmolada was also the location for some intense fighting in World War I reminders of which are constantly emerging as the glacier retreats. Before 1915 the Austro-Italian border crossed the Marmolada and it formed the frontline during the war. Fighting was continuous and to supply their troops the Austro-Hungarians built an under-ice city within the glacier which included 11km of tunnels. The frontline didn't move until the wider Italian front collapsed in late 1917.

The Rifugio Viel dal Pan (**www.rifugiovieldalpan.com**, tel 39 339 3865241) provides room-only accommodation and its excellent food and fabulous location make it a particularly busy venue in the summer especially as the Viel del Pan is popular with mountain bikers.

STAGE 19
Rifugio Viel dal Pan to Alleghe

Start	Rifugio Viel dal Pan (2435m)
Distance	24km
Ascent/Descent	230m/1670m
Difficulty	Moderate
Walking time	5hr 50min
Maximum altitude	2435m
Refreshments	There are lots of places to stop for refreshments or just rest and admire the view. In particular Rifugio Castiglioni, a historic hut on the north side of the Lago di Fedaia dam, has great views of the Marmolada and serves huge slabs of cheesecake. There are good lunch stops in Sottoguda.
Routefinding	Navigation isn't a problem and although the path is poorly defined on the ski-slopes it's impossible to get lost – just keep heading down.

After the last three days, Stage 19 almost feels like a day off. It's downhill all the way and, after the intensity of the journey across the Geisler Puez and Sella there is a distinct change of pace. The first 90min, finishing the contour walk along the grassy Viel del Pan and then descending to the Lago di Fedaia, are wonderful although the need to take photographs of the Marmolada's glacier is bound to slow things up.

om the Rifugio Viel dal Pan follow the Viel del Pan east ong Route 601. After 60min ignore the turn-off at the nction (**1**) with a path heading to the Rifugio La Gorza, d continue along the 601. Shortly afterwards you begin e steep descent down to the **Lago di Fedaia**.

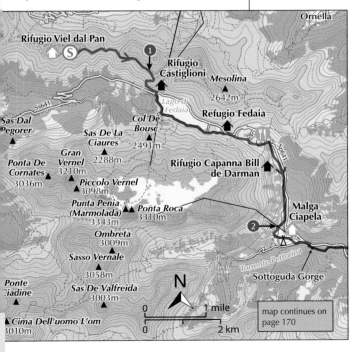

map continues on page 170

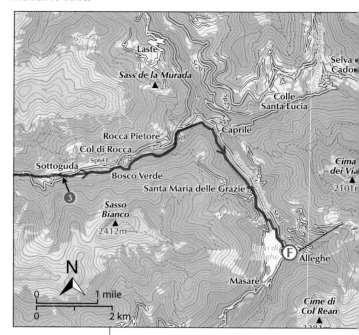

Accommodation and refreshments are available at the Rifugio Castiglioni (**www.rifugiomarmolada.it**, tel 39 0462 601117), originally an alpine association hut but now private. If you have time the World War I museum is worth a visit. It's full of artefacts, some of which have only recently been exposed by the retreating glacier.

Cross the dam and follow a concrete road east alon the southern shore of the Lago di Fedaia and past a se ond dam. Continue east to a car park and the **Refug Fedaia** (2050m) (www.rifugiofedaia.com, tel 39 43 0722007), a fairly modern ski hut, open in the summ which also provides accommodation.

From the hut head down a steep grassy ski slop along a poorly-defined path past the Ristorante B

*Descending to
Lago di Fedaia*

zzeria La Cianel. Continue down the ski slope for
nother 600m staying in the valley as it swings south. On
e other side of the road is the Rifugio Capanna Bill di
arman (www.capannabill.com, tel 39 0437 722100),
nother possible overnight on the way to Alleghe.

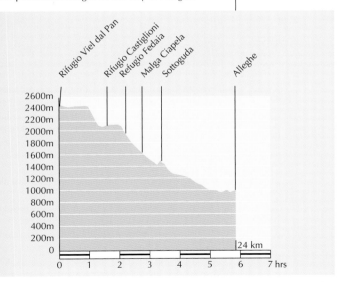

Sottoguda Gorge

Continue south down the little valley. The rate descent is now more gradual and the walking more comfortable. Roughly following the route of a ski draglift continue down for 30min (not on the main road) before turning west across a bridge (**2**) over a stream. Head south down to a concrete road (passing underneath a cable car) then east towards **Malga Ciapela** ski resort (1455m) Without going into the resort turn south towards a camp site and a stream, then head east to pick up the entry the **Sottoguda Gorge**.

Malga Ciapela has a range of services including a super-market, cashpoint and accommodation. It's the point at which the Traumpfad says goodbye to the Alta Via 2, which continues its journey round the Marmolada to the Pass San Pellogrino.

To get into the **Sottoguda Gorge** you have to pay (€3.5 – one way). This is the only toll you have to pay on the whole of the Traumpfad. A little train-like vehicle (a bus disguised as a train) chugs its way up and down the gorge (but you won't be walking 'all the way' if you take it!). The gorge, a narrow vertical gash in the landscape, is 2.2km long and picturesque Sottoguda at the bottom is a significant tourist trap. In the winter, when the numerous waterfalls freeze, it attracts ice climbers.

Sottoguda is a good place to stop for lunch. It has several restaurants and four hotels. The Hotel La Montanara (**www.lamontanara.it**, tel 39 0437 722017) and the Hotel Garni Al Serrai (**www.aiserrai.com**, tel 43 772 2120) are on the main street which you reach as you emerge from the gorge. The village has some perfectly preserved old timber farmhouses and other buildings– watch out for the mannequins dressed in traditional costumes; some of them are armed.

Continue through **Sottoguda** village to the main road, cross the bridge (**3**) (1300m) and pick up the riverside walk which starts in trees from the car park after the bridge. Following the Sottoguda-Masare Nature Route, the walk is well signed and stays on the same side of the river until it crosses a footbridge just north of **Alleghe**. It's essentially a flat 9km walk and takes around 2hr 30min. If stops are needed the best place is either at Saviner di

Alleghe (Photo: Max and Frances Harre)

Laste/Caprile, where the River Petterina meets the m
larger River Cordevole, or further south at Santa M
delle Grazie.

The scenery gets progressively better as you
closer to Alleghe with the huge cliffs of Civetta tower
menacingly over the valley.

ALLEGHE 979M

Alleghe is beautifully located and sits on a lake nestling immediately beneath
the cliffs. It attracts tourists all year and, as well as skiing, hiking and mountain
biking, draws in people who want a trip across the lake on a pedalo or even (in a
warm summer) a swim. The lake, so important to the town as a tourist attraction
is actually the product of a natural disaster – a huge landslide in 1771 which
killed 49 people. As the waters rose attempts were made to remove the blockage
but the task was too large and too dangerous and today's lake is the result.

There is a good choice of accommodation either in Alleghe itself or further along
the lakeside. The upmarket Sport Hotel Europa (**www.sporthoteleuropa.com**, te
39 04 3752 3362), clearly visible on the approach to the town, is surprisingly
good value in the summer months. Alternatively try the Hotel Central Alleghe
(**www.hotelcentralealleghe.com**, tel 39 0437 523476).

4 ALLEGHE TO BELLUNO

Portela del Piazedel (Stage 22)

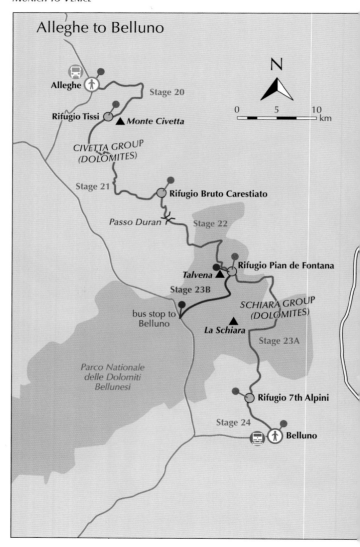

Alpine meadow and the Castello di Moschesin (Stage 22)

ection 4 completes the traverse of the Alps in great style and includes stretches of walking which are as memorable as any on the Traumpfad. Technically still part of the Dolomites it feels different. In particular it's quiet. The penultimate stage especially will be empty providing an experience which, in the context of the Alps, gets close to wilderness walking

After climbing up from Alleghe, the trail joins the Alta Via 1, which starts about five days north at Lago Braies near Dobbiaco, and follows it all the way to Belluno. This section can be broken into two legs. The first (Stages 20 and 21) makes the journey around the southwest flanks of Monte Civetta and passes immediately underneath its world-famous, 1200m-high and 6km-long western wall. On the far side of the Passo Duran, the second leg crosses the north eastern edges of the Parco Nationale delle Dolomiti Bellunesi, passing close by Talvena (2542m) via the Forcella de Zità Sud (2395m) and La Schiara (2565m). There is an option here for experienced via ferratists to take the Via Ferrata Marmol (grade 3C) straight over the top of La Schiara from the Forcella de la Vareta but this route is not described in detail here.

What unites both legs – particularly after the crowds on the Sella – is how quiet and empty they are. Even in August this section feels remote.

ACCESS AND ACCOMMODATION

Belluno is on the railway line with excellent connectivity by train or coach to Venice and other airports in northern Italy.

Apart from the start and finish a the accommodation in the final se tion is in mountain huts. Although little basic in terms of facilities the are friendly and, like most of th Italian huts, provide excellent food.

KEY INFORMATION

Distance	77km (or 59km walking following Stage 23B and skipping Stage 24)
Total ascent	6329m
Total descent	7810m
Alternative schedule	It is possible to avoid to drop a day (Stage 24) and avoid a relatively challenging day on Stage 23 by dropping down to the road and catching a bus to Belluno. Alternatively fast walkers of Stage 23 often choose to skip the night at Refugio 7th Alpini and head straight down to Belluno – but it makes for a huge day's walking. For walkers who don't mind not walking every step a completely different itinerary for this section would be to start by taking the lift up to Col dei Baldi (avoiding nearly 1000m of climb) from Alleghe, staying at Rifugio Vazzoler and then walking nine hours on to the Rifugio Sommariva al Pramperet. From there it's possible to get down to the road and catch the bus into Belluno.

STAGE 20
Alleghe to Rifugio Tissi

Start	Hotel Centrale, Alleghe (980m)
Distance	13km
Ascent/Descent	1780m/350m
Difficulty	Moderate
Walking time	6hr 10min
Maximum altitude	2260m
Refreshments	The Rifugio Adolfo Sonino al Coldai, at the end of all the big climbs, is ideally situated for a late lunch and serves fantastic strudel. The Refugio Tissi is fairly basic but it's very friendly and in a fantastic location.
Variant	Cable car from Alleghe to Col dei Baldi or chairlift from Alleghe to Lago Coldai, both cutting out almost all of the ascent, or a 'challenging', direct climb from Piani de Pezze to Lago Coldai.

It's a 1000m climb up from Alleghe and much of it is in trees and along ski runs but there are alternatives for those who don't mind getting a lift or are experienced enough to tackle the climb directly up to Lago Coldai. The second stage of the cable car starts at Piani de Pezze so a partially cable car-assisted ascent could be combined with the more direct route.

The most direct route involves fixed ropes, is subject to rock falls and is not recommended for less experienced walkers. It also misses out on some great views of Monte Pelmo, the 'most beautiful mountain in the Dolomites'.

Catching the chairlift (as opposed to the cable car) up from Alleghe makes for a very short day and only makes sense if you intend to go beyond Rifugio Tissi.

⊃m near the appropriately-named Hotel Centrale head ▶rth along the main road and turn right into the Via ℠ide de Gasperi. Stay on this road for nearly a kilome- as it switchbacks its way (three times) east to the edge town. Before passing the last house (**1**) leave the road

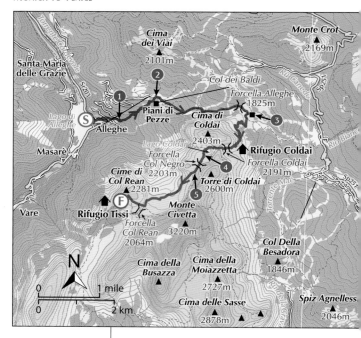

as it swings north and head east onto a track (marke
the 564). Climb through trees up the Val de Molin an
emerge, after 90min, at the **Piani di Pezze** (**2**) (1480m).

Head southeast underneath a cable car along
dirt road between trees and follow it for 3km up to th
Forcella Alleghe (1825m) where the route joins the Al
Via 1. ◀

The alternative,
tougher path,
follows Route 4 from
Piani di Pezze.

The views across the Val di Zoldo to **Monte Pelmo**
(3169m) are wonderful. Although not the highest
mountain in the Dolomites, its isolation makes it
one of the most prominent. It was climbed for the
first time in 1857 by John Ball, an Irishman who
later became the president of the British Alpine

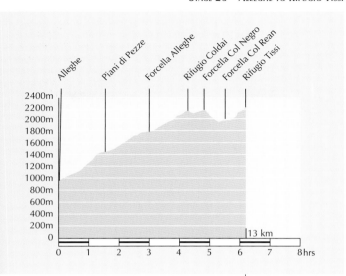

Club. When he climbed it it still had a significant glacier, only traces of which remain today.

From the Forcella Alleghe follow the Alta Via 1 signs west and then south along a track. After 200m, near some buildings (**3**) turn right onto a stony path (now the 556) that switchbacks its way up the mountain side in a west-erly direction. ▸ After 30min the path levels out and joins a broad path going south along the eastern flank of **Cima di Coldai** (2403m). After another 15 min the path swings west into a gully and, after climbing out past cables for a goods lift, makes the final approach to the **Rifugio Coldai** (2132m).

You can cut up across the switchbacks if you wish.

The Rifugio Adolfo Sonino al Coldai (tel 39 0473 789160), a CAI hut, is the ideal place for a lunch stop. It's a popular hut and much favoured by Civetta climbers.

181

From the refuge head west on a well-worn path up to a pass, the **Forcella Coldai** (2191m). Immediately below is the little glacial lake of **Lago Coldai**, beyond that the deep Valle Cordevole and beyond that Marmolada and the Sella Group. Immediately to the south are the first pinnacles of the Civetta west wall – Torre di Coldai, Torre Alleghe and the Torre Val Grande.

The **Civetta** group of mountains is a magnet for climbers and one of the most impressive, secluded ranges in the Dolomites. It's long and thin, running north–south with the deep valleys on either side: the Valle Cordevole (West) and the upper Val di Zoldo (East). The most impressive feature is the huge grey west wall, vertical cliffs over 1200m high and 6km long. The high point is Monte Civetta (3220m) itself first climbed in 1867 by the British mountaineer Francis Fox Tuckett, a central figure in the 'golden age of Alpinism' and one the first to climb in the Dolomites.

Lago Coldai

From the pass head down to the lake and follow route 560 around its right-hand side. Ignore the turnoff down to Alleghe, the arrival point for the alternative route from Piani di Pezze (**4**). Continue south, southwest along a stony path and climbing to a saddle, the **Forcella Col Negro** (2203m) with perhaps the best views of the great west wall. Take the right-hand fork (**5**) and ignore the route running immediately below the cliff. ▶ Follow the path down over scree across a boulder-strewn bowl.

The route below is hazardous because of the risk of falling rocks.

To the east is the huge 1200m high wall. Ahead on the southern side of the bowl is another small ridge the Forcella Col Rean (2064m). On the western end of this ridge, 90min away, is the dramatically-located Rifugio Tissi (2260m). Pray for good weather. The view of the **setting sun** at the Rifugio Tissi with the Marmolada and Sella to the west, and the changing colours of the west wall of the Civetta to the east is one of the Traumpfad's most memorable highlights.

For **Rifugio Tissi** turn right and climb for 200m to one of the most beautifully located huts between Munich and Venice.

Rifugio Tissi (tel 39 0437 721644) enjoys a stunning location that, along with a friendly atmosphere and good food, more than compensates for some fairly basic facilities. If your target is Rifugio Vazzoler then continue south over the Forcella Col Rean on Route 560.

STAGE 21
Rifugio Tissi to Rifugio Bruto Carestiato

Start	Rifugio Tissi (2250m)
Distance	16km
Ascent/Descent	740m/1160m
Difficulty	Challenging
Walking time	6hr
Maximum altitude	2260m
Refreshments	Stop for mid-morning refreshments at the Rifugio Vazzoler.
Routefinding	The route is straightforward although watch out for the patches of snow that can linger throughout year on the flanks of the Moiazza. The path is well defined and waymarking excellent.

Stage 21 completes the journey around the southwest corner of Civetta – a beautiful walk. Navigation is straightforward: just keep the cliffs on your left hand side.

At the end of the western wall the route swings east over a low pass and around the Torre Venezia (2337m), a stunning tower and a big attraction for climbers. The route then turns south around a huge bowl formed by Monte Civetta and Moiazza, before crossing a saddle and dropping down to the Rifugio Bruto Carestiato.

Alternative accommodation is available 40min further down the trail on the Passo Duran at the Refugio San Sebastiano, a small and very friendly hotel. Staying here would make the next day, an otherwise gruelling 8hr, a little easier.

After retracing your steps a short distance from Refugio Tissi (**1**) take a right fork and a different route down to the AV1 and Route 560. Head southwest along a stony path into a grassy bowl dotted with dwarf pine. After 800m (**2**) the route joins a path (Route 563) from the northwest and climbing up from Alleghe, and continues south

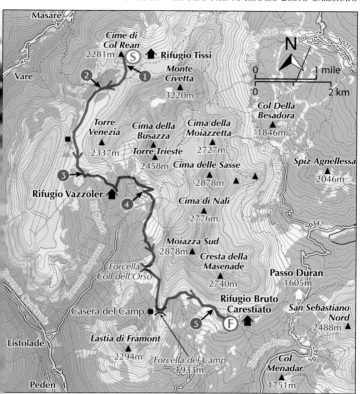

into pastures and past the Cason di Col Rean, ruins of a farmhouse. ▸

Continue southeast for 2km crossing a low pass and descend gently down to a dirt track. Follow it south then east, ignoring a turnoff to a farmstead (**3**), through trees to the **Rifugio Vazzoler** (1714m) reached between 1hr 30min and 2hr after leaving Refugio Tissi.

The atmospheric Rifugio Vazzoler is a place where climbers congregate to ascend the **Torre Venezia**

Ahead is the Torre Venezia, a final sentinel of the west wall of the Civetta with huge great boulders, like discarded building blocks, scattered around the low valley.

185

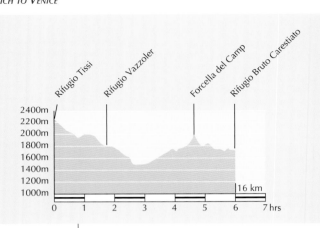

and the **Torre Trieste** (across the Val dei Cantoni immediately to the east). Val dei Cantoni runs north up the Civetta and separates two ridges running south and southwest from the centre of the massif. The Torre Venezia sits on the end of the southwestern ridge and its more delicate cousin, the Torre Trieste, sits on the end of the southern ridge. The Torre Trieste features some of the toughest climbs in the Dolomites.

The west wall of the Civetta

Shrouded in trees Rifugio Vazzoler (tel 39 0437 660008) doesn't enjoy the views of the Rifugio Tissi or the Refugio San Sebastiano but provides an option for walkers who want to go further than Rifugio Tissi on Stage 20.

From Rifugio Vazzoler rejoin the gravel road and follow it down through conifers northeast and then east. After an easy descent the route completes a double switchback reaching a gravelly gully after 2km (1430m) (**4**). Here it leaves the road, crosses the gully, joins Route 554 and heads south towards the magnificent western wall of the Moiazza.

If, as some argue, the **Moiazza** is separate to the Civetta, it is definitely overshadowed by its more famous neighbour. Its western wall is shorter and not as high. But it is still a wonderful walk and, with a mix of ancient pine, scree, and even snowfields, more varied.

Follow the 554 south, through pine trees and across three gullies, for a kilometre. After the third gully and still mainly in trees start a 200m climb, emerging after 800m under the wall of the Moiazza itself. Here there could be a snowfield and care needs to be taken on the last part up to the **Forcella Col dell'Orso** (1750m). The path now swings south and, after a short stretch of cable-assisted walking, descends gently along an easy path near to the Casera del Camp ruins. Ignoring a Route 552 turn-off, turn left and southeast up a grassy slope with distinctive red soil to **Forcella del Camp** (1933m), a saddle immediately underneath the Moiazza Sud.

From the pass head northeast down a path before swinging east under the south facing flank of the **Moiazza Sud**. Ahead, on a promontory, the **Rifugio Bruto Carestiato** (1834m) should be clearly visible. After emerging from a mountainside forest of larch the routes swings around across scree before turning (**5**) onto a final wooded ascent up to the refuge, about 60min from Forcella del Camp.

Rifugio Bruto Carestiato (**www.rifugiocarestiato.com**, tel 39 0437 62949) is a comfortable hut with accommodation organised in four bunked rooms. The food is good, particularly the Carestiato cake. One of its unique attractions is access to the Ferrata Constantini which starts just 10min away and goes up to the summit of Moiazza. It is considered to be the toughest via ferrata in the Dolomites.

STAGE 22

*Rifugio Bruto Carestiato to
Rifugio Pian de Fontana*

Start	Rifugio Bruto Carestiato (1835m)
Distance	20km
Ascent/Descent	1200m/1300m
Difficulty	Challenging
Walking time	8hr
Maximum altitude	2400m
Refreshments	The small friendly Rifugio Sommariva, 10min off the route and positioned just before the challenging second half of the day, provides the ideal lunch stop.
Routefinding	The AV1 route is well marked and easy to follow.
Variant	In bad weather head down from Passo Duran to the bus at Agordo.

Stage 22 heads into the heart of the Belluno Dolomites National Park. It is particularly peaceful, empty and very beautiful. It's definitely a day to be savoured, and the homely, slightly basic Rifugio Pian de Fontana is a good place to share what could be a last drink with Traumpfad companions before people separate on the various optional routes into Belluno.

From Rifugio Bruto Carestiato head northeast then ea
along a gravel track. Ahead and to the east of the Pass
Duran is the sheer west-facing flank of **Cima Nord di Sa**

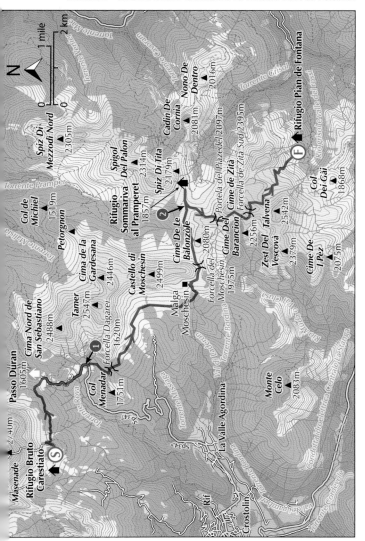

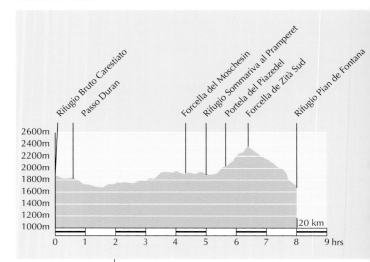

Sebastiano (2488m). It takes 40min to get down to the Passo Duran (1605m) which divides the Moiazza group in the northwest and the Pramper group of Dolomites in the southeast.

There are two private refuges at the Passo Duran. The Refugio San Sebastiano (www.passoduran.it, tel 37 0437 62360) and the Refugio Passo Duran (www.rifugiopassoduran.it, tel 39 3464 165461) are both halfway between a refuge and a small hotel and offer dormitory and private room accommodation.

From the pass walk south along the road for 1.7km and as the road crosses a stream, enter a car park on the left with information boards (1) (1520m). From the car park follow a forest path southeast then south, climbing steadily along Route 543 for about 800m to the Forcella Dagarei (1620m). Ignore the signed turn to the Col Menadar, continue on the 543 and, shortly after the signed turn, swing east. Within 300m the path emerges

om the conifers into a huge upland basin and a world of
vhite scree and dwarf pine.

The **basin** is formed by the southern flank of the
twin towered Tamer (the Tamer Davanti (2496m)
and the Tamer Grande (2547m)) and the western
flank of the Castello di Moschesin (2499m).

Continue for 1.6km along a fairly level rocky path.
he path swings south and starts a steady climb. After
km and 150m of ascent the route reaches the **Malga**
1oschesin (1800m) an emergency shelter with water
earby. ▶

*If the weather is clear
the glacier on the
Marmolada should be
visible to the west.*

From Malga Moschesin continue east along the 543
nd follow switchbacks climbing up to the pass, **Forcella**
el Moschesin (1975m) and a meadow full of alpine
owers.

To the right of the path are abandoned barracks.
Directly ahead lies the **Val Balanzola**, and the cliffs
of the Castello di Moschesin rise to the left.

*Castello di Moschesin
and the Val Balanzola*

The views north from this path along the Val Balanzola to Monte Pelmo are excellent.

There are two routes at the pass. Take the one neare the barracks. Follow it east as it climbs up a little gorge along the side of a ridge and then down along an undu lating grassy path to the **Rifugio Sommariva al Prampere** (1857m). ◀

The Rifugio Sommariva al Pramperet (**www. rifugiosommarivaalpramperet.it**, tel 39 437 1956153.) is a tiny hut (only 30 places), low on facilities but high on charm. Arrive in good time to guarantee a helping of the soup of the day.

From Rifugio Sommariva al Pramperet head bac along the Route 543 to a junction (**2**) with the 514. Tur left at this junction and go south, climbing gently up stony path through dwarf pine. Ahead to the left is th Cime di Zità (2461m), its west-facing cliff marking th start point of the glacier (only recently disappeared) th carved out the huge valley below. Emerging from th dwarf pine the path swings west and climbs steeply up a saddle, the **Portela del Piazedel** (2097m).

Approaching the Forcella de Zità Sud

After the Portela del Piazedel follow the path south east climbing gently across a wide limestone expanse

the east are the walls of the Cime di Zità and to the
uth a ridge. The route heads south and takes an increas-
gly steep path that turns into a scramble before the final
assy stretch up to the **Forcella de Zità Sud** (2402m).

The views from the pass are immense. Some claim
that it is possible to see the **Adriatic** and Venice, but
this may be a mountain myth and even without a
silvery twinkle in the distance, the view is compel-
ling. If there is time drop your bag and make the
easy 10min climb south to Talvena (2452m).

Crossing a pass often feels like entering a new
world and it is particularly the case at the Forcella
de Zità Sud. What had been a harsh north-facing
dry limestone landscape is replaced by the lush
green and grassy world of the Van de Zita de Fora.
Whistling marmots signal your approach and, if it's
sunny, snakes may be soaking up heat on the rocks.
Only the unlucky will miss out on the herds of
chamois. The white outline of the path marks a long
inviting descent. After escaping the initial shadow
of Talvena, the wonderful valley views are further
improved by sight of the last Alpine mountains on
the Traumpfad, the Schiara.

It takes about 90min to drop 750m down the only
th to the **Rifugio Pian de Fontana** (1632m). The final
scent to the hut is particularly steep and at the end of a
ng day care should be taken.

The Refugio Pian de Fontana (tel 39 335 609 6819) is
a lovely hut where the relaxed atmosphere, good food
and helpful management make up for the cramped
conditions and primitive facilities. The staff gleefully
inform you that the showers are free and that there is
no hot water.

RIFUGIO PIAN DE FONTANA TO BELLUNO

Approaching the Forcella de la Vareta

At this point in Section 4 you have to make a choi‹ Because of a landslide in 2009 a route which previou‹ went east around the Schiara to Rifugio 7th Alpini ‹ closed and the only option was to climb over the ‹ along a route that required via ferrata gear and expe‹ ence. This eastern route is now open again (and describ‹ here as Stage 23A) but is not yet included in the Germ‹ guides and therefore rarely used and challenging to f‹ low. German walkers either go over the top along ‹ via ferrata or head down a valley to the northwest of ‹ Schiara and catch a bus to Belluno (Stage 23B); catchi‹ the bus is the most popular German option.

The author walked Stage 23A in 2015 and Stage 2‹ in 2014 but has not as yet completed the via ferrata rou‹ (which comes off Stage 23A). An alternative source ‹ information for that route is identified below.

If you'd rather do the via ferrata route then consider staying at the Refugio San Sebastiano on Passo Duran. The manager is very helpful and via ferrata gear, booked ahead, can be hired and dropped off further along the route (currently you can do it at Tarzo, two days after Belluno, although this arrangement may vary).

Catching the bus to Belluno reduces the number of days required for this Section from five to four (skipping Stage 24).

STAGE 23A
Rifugio Pian de Fontana to Rifugio 7th Alpini

Start	Rifugio Pian de Fontana (1630m)
Distance	14km
Ascent/Descent	2200m/2100m
Difficulty	Challenging
Walking time	8hr
Maximum altitude	1830m
Refreshments	There is nowhere on the route for refreshments and a picnic is needed for a journey which is likely to take at least 8hr.
Routefinding	The route has only recently been re-waymarked but with current levels of use it's not as well defined as other Traumpfad paths and where it's overgrown the waymarks can be hard to spot.

This stage takes a clockwise route around the mountain range. After a significant initial loss of altitude, it climbs over three passes. It's a tough walk and compared to the rest of the Munich to Venice route crosses landscape that is particularly empty.

Much of the route up to the first pass, the Forcella Torond, is in trees and includes short cable and ladder-assisted stretches. Once on the pass, and for 50m only, the path is open and exposed and would be challenging in poor weather. Finally the descent from the third pass, just before the final approach to the Refugio 7th Alpini is steep, unpleasant and caution is needed.

Given the limited use the route has got in the recent past check with the manager at the Rifugio Pian de Fontana for updates. The manager should know its current status.

If you are planning to get to Belluno today then there are two alternative ways down. The shortest of the two shortcuts means leaving the route some 2hr before the end so it should be possible to get to Belluno from the Rifugio Pian de Fontana in about 10hr 30min.

Casera Dei Ranchi

From the Rifugio Pian de Fontana follow the 514 south on a steep switchbacking descent through beech trees. At the bottom of the valley (**1**) leave the 514 (which continues up to the pass, the Forcella de la Vareta) and head down and east on the 520. After 15min the path reaches the **Casera dei Ranchi**, an unsupported refuge. Crossing from one side of the valley to the other continue down for 50min to a footbridge (**2**), cross it and follow a road on the other side.

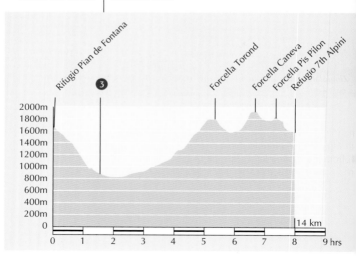

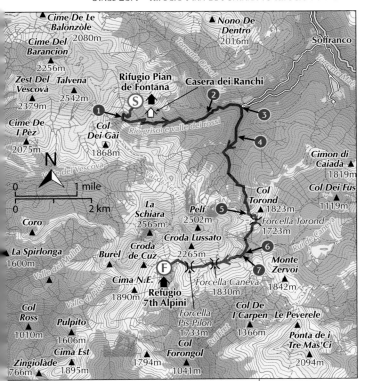

After about 1.4km (680m) (**3**) turn right off the road and join the 527, following a route signed to the Refugio 7th Alpini. After a further 800m cross another footbridge (**4**) from the right to left-hand side of a stream and continue south along a path that gradually loses definition.

For the next 2hr **progress will be slow**. Stretches of the route are steep and fixed steel cables and wooden ladders are needed to overcome the toughest sections. The path is occasionally overgrown and the waymarks hard to locate.

Descending from the Forcella Torond

After a 900m climb the 527 emerges above the treeline (**5**) (1575m) in open ground below the towering cliffs of **Pelf** (2502m). Head south across the open ground before swinging east and climbing onto the pass. The waymarks before the pass, the **Forcella Torond** (1723m), are particularly obscure but its location is clear enough.

The second of these junctions, with the 507, offers the shortcut down to the Stage 24 route to Belluno.

At the pass head south along a flat but exposed path marked to Refugio 7th Alpini and down into a grassy gully. Follow the path along the gully into beech trees and past the first of two junctions (**6** and **7**) with paths turning left. ◄

Emerging from the trees the path now zig-zigs its way up an increasingly tight and steep gully to the second and highest pass, the **Forcella Caneva** (1830m). After crossing the pass, continue east across a grassy but happily shallow valley, past a junction with the 511 (also heading down to Belluno) to the third and final pass, the **Forcella Pis Pilon** (1733m). The descent from this pass surprisingly steep with loose limestone pebbles making the going treacherous. Arriving at the beautifully located **Refugio 7th Alpini** (1493m) is a relief as well as a pleasure.

The Refugio 7th Alpini (**www.rifugiosettimoalpini. com**, tel 39 437 94 16 31) is another relaxed Italian hut positioned at the head of a valley. A popular destination for mountain bikers it serves excellent hearty food.

STAGE 23B

Rifugio Pian de Fontana to Belluno

Start	Rifugio Pian de Fontana to Belluno (1630m)
Distance	10km
Ascent/Descent	120m/1650m
Difficulty	Moderate
Walking time	4hr 40min
Maximum altitude	1705m
Refreshments	Mid-morning refreshments can be taken at the Rifugio Furio Bianchet.
Routefinding	The long descent along the forest road can be mesmerising and the path, which cuts across switchbacks, is easily missed.

An hourly bus service (Line 01-I) is scheduled from Agordo (about 10km to the north of the bus stop) to Belluno (www.dolomitibus.it) and the manageress at the Rifugio should be able to provide timetable information. After crossing the pass most of the walk follows a forest road along a valley although the final descent to the main road is a steep one.

s with Stage 23A leave the refuge and head south on the 4 on a switchback trail down the hillside but instead turning left at the junction with the 520 (1600m) (**1**),

The view down the valley from the Forcella de la Vareta

continue with the 514. As the path reaches the bottom the valley and the head of the stream there may be ice from the previous winter to cross. Follow 514 up throu

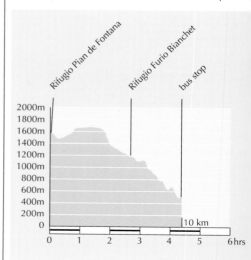

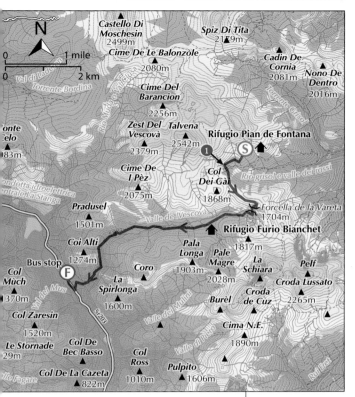

es on a 150m climb southeast along an increasingly
tty but exposed path to the **Forcella de la Vareta**
'04m). Just beyond the pass the route reaches the junc-
n with the via ferrata path heading over the Schiara.

The via ferrata element of the Schiara traverse to
Rifugio 7th Alpini known as the **via ferrata Marmol**
involves crossing a pass, the Forcella Marmol. In
terms of Italian via ferrata grading system it is a 3C,
which makes it a route of moderate difficulty. The

via ferrata Marmol takes 2hr 30min to cross and this part of the route is described (as BELLO4 and 5) in Cicerone's *Via Ferrata of the Italian Dolomites Vol 2*, by Graham Fletcher and John Smith (currently being updated for 2019). Appropriate equipment is essential, as is good weather. Although substantially tougher than anything that has gone before the consensus is that Traumpfad walkers – walkers who have coped with the Friesenbergscharte and the Birkkarspitz – should be able to manage the crossing, providing that there someone in the group with previous via ferrata experience who is willing to take a lead.

Turn right and follow a path (now the 518) into tr descending around the head of the valley. After a desc of nearly 450m the path joins a forest road leading to **Rifugio Furio Bianchet** (1246m) (tel 39 335 644 69 which has accommodation.

The drop from the Rifugio to the road and the stop (450m) is nearly 800m. Although it is possible walk all the way along the forest road the path of takes a more direct route across switchbacks in the ro The mesmerising effect of walking along the forest r means that these shortcuts are easily missed. When reach the main road, turn right and walk about half a ometre to find your bus stop. See the end of Stage 24 information about Belluno.

STAGE 24

Rifugio 7th Alpini to Belluno

Start	Rifugio 7th Alpini (1495m)
Distance	14km
Ascent/Descent	280m/1250m
Difficulty	Easy
Walking time	4hr 20min
Maximum altitude	1495m

After handling the Schiara traverse the descent to Belluno holds no challenges. The first half is a pleasant walk down a steep-sided wooded valley and the second a walk along roads through villages and the northern suburbs of Belluno. This stage is short so if time allows stop for a dip in the pool at the bottom of the initial descent. It's the best place to have a swim on the whole Traumpfad.

Join the 501 and follow a well-defined engineered path zig-zagging its way down a gorge through a beech forest. After descending for nearly 300m in just over a kilometre the path hits the valley bottom where there is a lovely series of cascading waterfalls (**1**) feeding a pool and providing the perfect spot for a swim.

Now on the right-hand side of the valley continue south along the path. Still descending steeply cross back to the valley's left-hand side and ignore paths joining from the left after 2km and 2.2km. The second of these paths (**2**), marked the 507, is where the shortcut from towards the end of Stage 23A rejoins the main route.

After crossing a bridge, **Ponte del Marino** (681m), and returning to the right-hand side of the valley the path surprisingly starts to climb and, still in beech forest, gets high above the gorge. Another 2km after crossing the bridge, and after passing information boards (**3**)

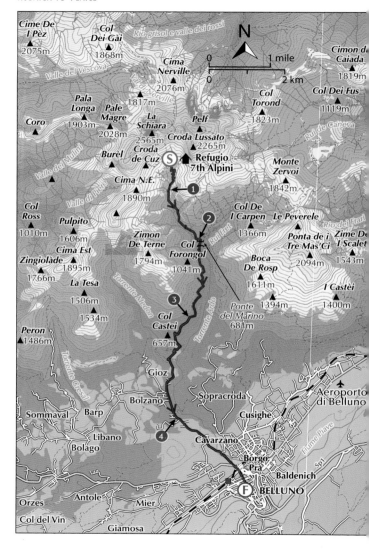

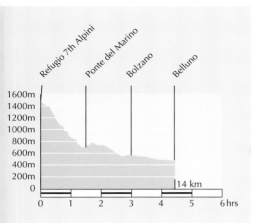

describing how the gorge was formed, the path turns into a dirt road and then a metalled road.

Continue south along the road passing a several scattered and attractive looking farmsteads to the little village of **Gioz** and then the slightly more substantial **Bolzano** (541m). From Bolzano continue south along the road for .9km where the road forks (**4**). Take the quieter left-hand fork, and after 300m join a footpath near a tennis centre. After another 200m or so this rejoins a road that continues into the centre of **Belluno**.

BELLUNO 443M

With a population of 36,000, Belluno is largest town visited since Munich but it's hardly a metropolis. Sheltering beneath the Dolomites it's kept apart from the Venetian plain by a final ridge of mountains to the southwest. It sits on the junction of the Piave, which dominates much of the rest of the walk to Venice, and the much smaller Torrento Ardo. The old centre of the town, on a ridge above the Piave, is particularly attractive and includes several fine Renaissance and Baroque buildings including a 17th-century cathedral and the 15th-century Palazzo dei Rettori.

Although there are plenty of places to eat, particularly in the old part of town, there is a limited choice of hotels. For value stay at the Casa per Ferie 'Al Centro' (**www.centrocongressibelluno.it/casa.html**, tel 39 437 944 460), a youth hostel or, slightly more upmarket, the Albergo Cappello (**www.albergocappello.com**, tel 39 437 940246). Both places are located in the streets immediately to the north of the main square (just north of the historic centre), the Parco di Piazza dei Marti.

5 BELLUNO TO VENICE

In the beech trees near the San Mamante (Stage 25)

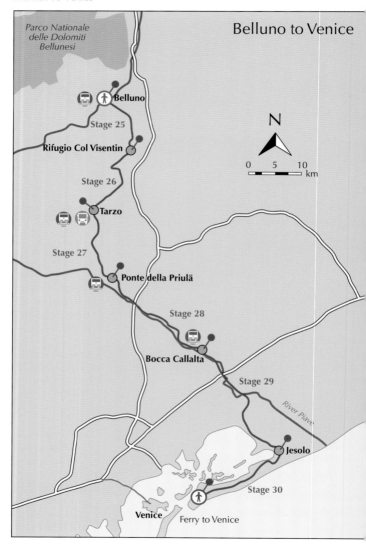

On the bank of the Fiume Sile (Stage 30)

From Belluno, Venice is still six days away including four days across the flat Venetian plain. After sharing much of the journey with other long-distance routes (such as the Alta Via 1 and 2) the Traumpfad is, unsurprisingly, on its own from Belluno to Venice (and it shows in the waymarking). It's not great walking but it has to be done to complete your epic journey.

There are stretches of road walking which can be very hot and, at the wrong time of day and in sheltered spots near water and trees, mosquitoes take no prisoners. But there are compensations. The route offers a World War I history lesson, the food is excellent (particularly the ice cream) and prosecco is the local beverage.

And the biggest compensation must be Venice itself which, despite the crowds, must be the most beautiful city in the world in which to finish a walk.

Before reaching the Venetian plain there is one last climb to complete: the last mountain, on top of which is the last hut, Refugio Col Visentin (1764m). After a splendid ridge walk, with great views back into the Dolomites, the route descends to Revine and onto Tarzo (great accommodation at the Albergo Ai Pini) before reaching the River Piave the next day. It then follows the Piave east, walking along levées above the flood plain and across fields of maize, grapes and beans. After the seaside resort of Jesolo it turns south along the western side of the sand spit dividing the Venice Lagoon from the Adriatic before crossing by ferry to Venice itself.

The plain around the Piave is perfectly flat. Much of it is reclaimed marshland. The towns, many devastated in both world wars, are nearly all centred around churches with enormously tall elegant church towers visible from a great distance across the flat landscape. These towers imitate the style of the Campanile, the most copied church tower in the world, in St Mark's Square and mark the route all the way to Venice.

Groups of walkers formed in the journey across the Alps melt away in the heat of the Venetian plain. Thos with time commitments (younge walkers predominantly) often get bus or train near Tarzo. Many stic with it, however, and a rucksacke silhouette in the distance, trudgin along the top of a levée, is almost ce tainly, like you, finishing its journe from Munich to Venice.

ACCOMMODATION

Accommodation on the last sectio is good and, apart from a decidedl quirky hut on the first night, is in sma hotels some of which provide partic larly good food.

KEY INFORMATION

Distance	144km
Total ascent	2380m
Total descent	2870m
Alternative schedule	To cut short the flat finale of the Venetian plain, you could catch a bus from Tarzo.

STAGE 25

Belluno to Rifugio Col Visentin

Start	Piazza Duomo, Belluno (400m)
Distance	17km
Ascent/Descent	1600m/270m
Difficulty	Moderate
Walking time	5hr 30min
Maximum altitude	1765m
Refreshments	The best place for a lunch stop is in the little ski resort of Nevegal where there are a couple of restaurants and a hotel. The Bar La Grava, further up the hill, is not always open.
Routefinding	Generally good although the route amongst the ski runs just beyond Nevegal can be a little hard to find.
Variant	Avoid some road walking and detour via Caleipo.

The last climb of the Traumpfad, the final pull up to the Rifugio Col Visentin, is the sting in the tail of what is otherwise an easy walk. The rewards, however – amazing views back into the Dolomites and a night in a decidedly quirky hut – are well worth the effort.

Two routes are described below. The original route bypasses Caleipo and continues on the road up to the Santuario di San Mamante. The alternative (which in wet weather can be muddy) avoids the road and goes through Caleipo to rejoin the route 90min later. The alternative is more scenic and in good weather there is an opportunity for a swim. It also seems to be the one that is now signed and that the locals are encouraging walkers to follow.

nd the beautiful Piazza Duomo in the centre of Belluno. ear the tourist information office you will find the only scalator on your mountain pilgrimage. Take the escalator own to the car park below town (**1**). Turn left to follow a otpath, staying on the northern side of the Piave, to the econd, older bridge, Ponte della Vittoria. Cross the bridge nd on the other side, following Munich–Venice signs to

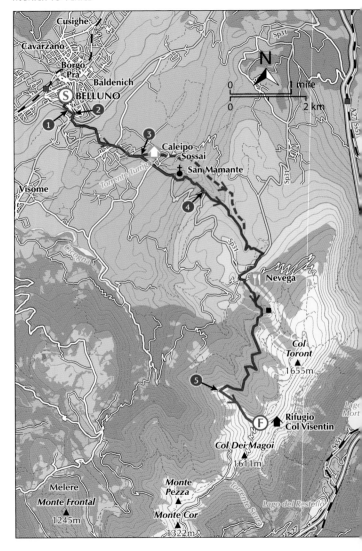

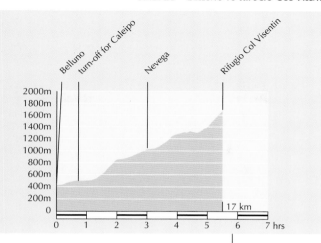

ifugio Col Visentin, turn left before the Albergo Al
onte della Vittoria into Via Marcello Miari. After about
00m along a small road (**2**) turn right, cross over the
ia Vincenzo Lante and head southeast and then east for
00m to the Via Sanfor. Go east-southeast along the Via
anfor for 500m to the Via Edmondo de Amicis and fol-
w it east for another 1.5km (**3**).

ariant via Caleipo

rn left here and head into **Caleipo** where there are sev-
al bars. Go east along the Via San Mamante and, as it
rns north, continue east to the village of **Sossai**. From
e square in front of church descend gently along the
ad between the church and fountain as the metalled
ad turns to gravel. Continue uphill past a house, cross
meadow and enter trees. At a fork follow the Munich–
nice sign and turn left arriving at some beautiful pools
the river – an inviting spot for a dip. Cross the stream,
mb steeply up a path to a cable-supported section and
en continue over a grassy clearing into a meadow.

   Keep to right side of the meadow and go back into
 forest, following the red-yellow-red markings through

the trees. After a slight descent the path reaches a for
turns left and starts to climb again. After crossing nume
ous small streams the path reaches a stone house ar
heads down to cross a stream, then a second stream a
then climbs slightly to rejoin the original route. ◄

Main route continues

◄ For the original route bypassing Caleipo, continue c
the main road up a hill for another kilometre to whe
the road turns sharply south. On the far side of the ro
is the Santuario di San Mamante (510m). Continue sou
past the chapel and then turn left and east along a d
trail, an ancient road, and follow it as it climbs throu
beech trees. Continue southeast for a kilometre follo
ing a route, sometimes forest road, sometimes path, ov
grown at times, to a road (**4**). Cross the road, join a d
road (the Via San Mamante) and follow it southeast
3km to a main road. ◄

The variant route
comes in after
about 2km.

Turn right onto the main road and follow it as
swings up into the ski resort at **Nevega** (785m) whe
food can be found in one of the bars.

From Nevega cross the road to the bottom of the s
run and take Route 1 and Route 3 to Rifugio Col Visenti
Follow a dirt road up through trees to the Bar La Gra
(not usually open in the summer). Continue up across
clearing and follow Route 3 southwest. Ignore a turn
the left (Route 6) and take a beautifully engineered pa
almost perfectly contoured, that swings south along th
side of the valley for nearly 3km to meet a path climbi
up from the Belluno valley. After one final stretch of co
tour walking (now heading southwest along the side o
gully) the route emerges into open ground, benches a
a picnic table (**5**). ◄

The views across
the Val Belluno
to the Gruppo
Della Schiara are
wonderful and about
to get even better.

The route turns and makes the last tough ascent
the Traumpfad up to **Rifugio Col Visentin** (1764m). T
distinctive profile of the Dolomites that you can now s
includes its most iconic mountains, the Drei Zinnen (T
Cima).

The Rifugio Col Visentin (**www.rifugiocolvisentin.**
net, tel 39 0437 27110) is a strange but wonderful

place. The last hut on the route was one of first Italian huts to be constructed (built by an Italian born in Stoke Newington). It's also a lighthouse visible from the Adriatic and partly a memorial to the 5th Alpine Artillery Regiment. It's completely surrounded by communication towers which, as well contributing to a bizarre appearance, make it visible from miles away. Most of the accommodation is in dormitories but there is a smaller room that can be booked. The food is excellent as is the grappa, homemade and stored in large evil-looking bottles that surround the walls of the dining room. The hut is a big supporter of the Traumpfad and is the place to buy commemorative stickers and postcards – although with five days still to do you might feel that that would be tempting fate.

Lovely path up to Rifugio Col Visentin

STAGE 26
Rifugio Col Visentin to Tarzo

Start	Rifugio Col Visentin (1765m)
Distance	18km
Ascent/Descent	130m/1670m
Difficulty	Moderate
Walking time	5hr 40min
Maximum altitude	1765m
Refreshments	Rifugio Pian de le Femene offers excellent home-cooked local food and provides a great place to stop for a last meal in the mountains.
Routefinding	There are some helpful waymarks, particularly near the start where Munich–Venice signs and TV1 waymarks point the way. An easy turn to miss is the one at Forcella Zoppei by which time the mountain road will have had a hypnotic effect.
Variant	Wet weather road option down from Rifugio Pian de le Femene.

With all the climbing now out of the way there is now only one hill challenge left, the descent down to Revine, as you move dramatically from a mountain to a Mediterranean landscape.

The descent from Rifugio Pian de le Femene to Revine is steep and can be slippery if wet. This stretch can be avoided by following a road down from the Rifugio Pian de le Femene.

From Rifugio Col Visentin, go south on a mountain roa for 2.7km (some of the corners can be cut) to the **Forcel Zoppei** (**1**) (1417m). At this point the route leaves th road and joins a grassy path on the western side of th ridge.

Join a path heading southwest and connecting a seri of mini-summits along the ridgeline. After 1.5km, and gentle climb, the first summit, **Monte Pezza** (1436m),

Leaving the Rifugio Col Visentin (Photo: Max and Frances Harre

eached. From here swing southwest descending gently own to **Monte Cor** (1324m), a pond and a farmstead. ollow the farm access road southwest for 300m before eaving it as it turns east. Continue southwest descending ently across meadows for 2km to another farmstead, the **asere Frascon** (1174m). From here (marked Route 1033) 's just 30mins to **Rifugio Pian de le Femene** (1120m).

Rifugio Pian de le Femene (tel 39 0438 583645) is a tiny alberge with limited accommodation but excellent food. World War II memorabilia as well as the usual dead animals decorate the walls.

From the refuge follow Route 1032 down the moun- inside. Head south across a meadow into beech trees nd follow a well-defined rocky path. After descending 00m (over a distance of a kilometre) it joins a forest trail ut only stays with it, meandering, for 200m before part- g company again. Your path, the 1032, apart from some inor meanders, stays on a southeast course emerging nto a road and (probably) bright sunlight after 1hr.

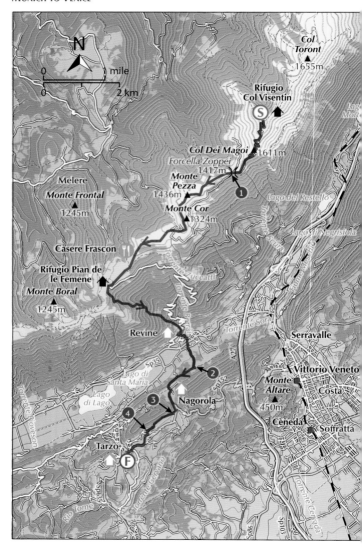

WET WEATHER ROAD ROUTE TO REVINE

To take the road from the Rifugio Pian de le Femene join the Via San Francesco from in front of the Rifugio and follow it east down the hill on long meandering route to Revine.

Ahead is the small town of Revine.

Revine's main claim to fame is two picturesque glacial lakes further down the valley. These may be visited if you don't mind walking on roads all the way to Tarzo. Revine has an upmarket hotel, Ai Cadelach Hotel Ristorante Benessere (**www.cadelach.it**, tel 39 0438 523010) located towards the Lago di Maria if you don't want to stay in Tarzo.

From the forest path turn right onto road, take e first left, and head down the Via Della Valla to e church. Turn right along Via San Matteo to Via

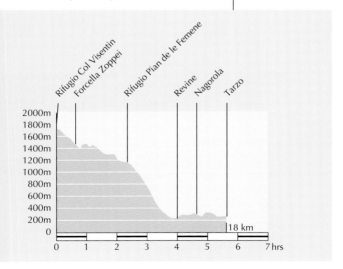

In a vineyard on the way to Tarzo

Somavilla. Turn right here, cross Via Maestra and head south along Via della Lama, cross the main road and continue south. Cross the next junction and head south past the old outdoor washing facilities on the edge of town. After 600m the road turns right (**2**). Continue southwest along a path (now designated Route 1052) and follow it for another 600m to a small road. Turn left and follow the road into the pretty little village of **Nagorola** (320m) which has a bar/restaurant Locanda Cordirosso and a bed and breakfast (La Nicchia, tel 39 0438 524098).

Go through Nagorola, take a right turn and continue south over a junction with a larger road. 200m after the junction (**3**) turn right onto an access road, and follow past houses onto a path. The path is shaded and can be muddy but follow it southwest to where it emerges above houses in a shallow valley. Continue south (**4**) down through the houses to the main road and follow it as it swings west into **Tarzo** (270m) about 900m away.

Tarzo is a small town and although it only has one hotel, the Albergo Ai Pini (**www.albergoaipini.it**, tel 39 04 3858 6206), it has a range of other services including cashpoint, post office and baker. The Albergo Ai Pini is a good quality family-run hotel in a beautiful 17th-century building with gardens overlooking the surrounding hills. It's a nice place with great food providing a touch of well-deserved luxury. It is situated on a low rise slightly south of the town centre. To get there, turn left just before the junction with the main road.

STAGE 27

Tarzo to Ponte della Priulä

Start	Albergo Ai Pini, Tarzo (275m)
Distance	29km; to Susegana: 27km
Ascent/Descent	550m/750m
Difficulty	Easy
Walking time	6hr 20min; to Susegana: 5hr 50min
Maximum altitude	300m
Refreshments	There are several options on the approach to Refrontolo and in Refrontolo itself.
Routefinding	There is little waymarking for Ponte della Priula but with long stretches along roads the route is fairly straightforward.
Variant	Finish at the more interesting town of Susegana.

Only four days to go but Stage 27 is the first of three really long stages. Over half of the day is spent pounding along hard surfaces, although thankfully the roads are not that busy. As you complete the transition from the rolling hills of the pre-Alps to the Venetian plain you walk the first of many kilometres along the tops of levées.

Ponte della Priulä is not an inspiring destination. It's a characterless one-street town, with just one plain (albeit good value, clean and comfortable) hotel, several adequate restaurants and numerous places to eat ice cream. The alternative destination, Susegana, is more interesting (with the remains of the Castello San Salvatore) and includes a more upmarket hotel, the Hotel Astoria. Getting there involves leaving the main route before it reaches the River Piave and makes for a slightly shorter day. Unfortunately this has to be paid for with an extra unpleasant extra 4km slog (or perhaps bus journey) along a road to Ponte della Priula on the next day.

ead northwest along the main road through Tarzo and
rn left past the large baroque church (**1**). Follow occa-
nal signs for Route 1051. Head south along the Via
jo descending gently and ignoring turn-offs to the left

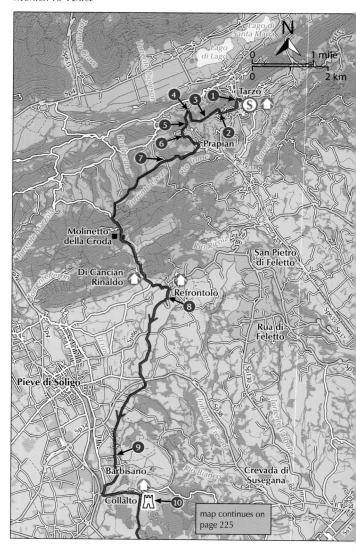

map continues on
page 225

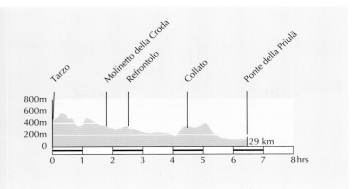

and right and continue southwest along a small road. After a kilometre, and just before reaching the last houses in the village, turn right onto a path (**2**) running uphill alongside a meadow into trees. As the path reaches the trees it swings, once again southwest. ▸

Be prepared: if the weather is humid this forest path is full of mosquitoes.

After 600m emerge from woods near a house (**3**) and follow a local road as it descends east and then swings north. After 100m take a sharp left (**4**) turn onto a track (there is an MV/1051 sign) and follow it down across a field and back into trees before emerging onto a road near houses (**5**). Continue past the houses onto a track (still 1051) and follow it down to another access road (**6**). Continue southeast on the access road down to the little village of **Prapian** (270m). At the junction in the centre of the village turn right onto a concrete road and stay on it for 1.2km as it climbs west out of a low valley.

At the top of the hill the concrete road reaches a junction with a larger tarmac road running north-south. Cross the junction (**7**) and follow an access road south-west for 2km. This part of the route was badly affected by flash flooding in 2014 and shifts between concrete, gravel and dirt roads as it finds its way through a pleasant agricultural landscape. After 2km the path swings south and 500m further on joins a road. Head south along the road to the **Molinetto della Croda**.

Molinetto della Croda

The Molinetto della Croda is a famous **watermill** that dates back to the 17th century and was still producing flour until the mid-20th century. But this attractive location has an unfortunate dark side. In August 2014, during the flash flood, a marquee containing a hundred men enjoying a party was hit by a five foot wave immediately in front of the mill. Four people were drowned and 20 injured.

From the Molinetto della Croda it's 2.5km south along a road to **Refrontolo** (205m). Fortunately refreshment options, distinctly lacking so far, become more frequent as you get close to the town. Unless you are carrying your lunch the opportunity should be grabbed as there is nowhere to stop after this until Barbisanello. The first place, the **Ristorante Il Buon Gustaio di Cancian Rinaldo**, is reached after 1.2km, and if it's hot will be a very welcome sight.

Refrontolo itself is a small town with two bar/restaurants, cashpoints and a shop. Between 1917

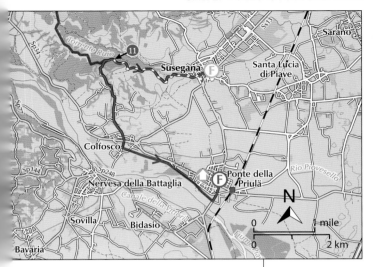

and 1918 it was the home of the Austro-Hungarian high command on the Piave front and features in a recent award-winning novel *Not all bastards come from Vienna*, a book about the front in the last years of World War I.

The next stretch, from Refrontolo to Barbisanello (a sprawling town) has nothing to redeem itself. It involves road walking on larger roads (thankfully not that busy) through bland countryside. The only consolation is knowing that this is the worst section on the whole route.

From the junction in the centre of Refrontolo follow e Via della Vitorria south. To cut out a long switchback the road turn right (**8**) after 200m and rejoin the main ad further down the hill. Head south along the main ad ignoring a right turn after 800m and after 2km pass derneath a dual carriageway. From the bridge over the al carriageway continue south for 2.4km through sub-bs to **Barbisano**. At the junction (**9**) local signs suggest a cross-country route to Collato (the next village) but unless the waymarking has improved this route is difficult to follow.

> If refreshments are needed desperately turn right at the junction and walk along the Via Kennedy, turn left and head to the church, opposite which is a bar and nearby also an ice-cream parlour (shut at lunchtime).

Continue south along the Via Piave until it reaches the Via Lierza. Carry on south at the junction to head down the Via Cimitero for 200m and as the road swings west join a small access road and then follow it south to the Via Piave and turn left. Turn left again at next junction and follow a road east for 600m to **Collato** (145m).

> The small village of Collato features the tower and other remains of a 14th-century **castle**. Bizarrely the castle and its nearby sister the Castello San Salvatora were seen as military targets by the Italian artillery and largely destroyed. The village has two restaurants if refreshments are needed.

Stay on the road through Collato and follow it as it swings south. The tarmac at last finishes and the route joins a pleasant gravel road (**10**) through vineyards, still going south. After 2.8km the gravel road joins a metalled road, the Via Tombola (**11**).

The castle remains at Collato

ternative finish at Susegana

finish the stage at Susegana, turn left onto the Via
mbola and follow it east for 3.5km. The Castello San
lvatora is on the western side of the town and the Hotel
toria (www.hotel-astoria.com, tel 39 0438 738525)
mediately to the north.

Turn left at the junction and head south, occasionally   Main route continues
utheast, for 2.7km passing through **Colfosco** on the
ay. Cross a major junction with a larger east/west run-
ng road and, after 200m, on the southern outskirts of
e town, turn left and east onto a levée. The River Piave
s now been reached and the levée is the only elevated
ature on what for the rest of the walk to Venice, is a
rfectly flat landscape.

The **River Piave** holds an almost sacred status in the
minds of Italian nationalists. In 1917 the Austro-
Hungarians broke the previous stalemate and the
12th Battle of Isonzo (also known as the Battle of
Caporetto) and the defeated Italian Army scattered.
With the whole of the northern plain exposed to
the combined Austro-Hungarian/German Army, the
retreating Italian Army somehow reformed and held
a defensive line at the River Piave. Like Dunkirk,
defeat was turned into a sort of victory.

The Piave gained further prominence in the
spring of 1918 when the Austro-Hungarian/German
attack, designed to coincide with the Ludendorff
offensive on the western front, was repelled.
Months later, at the Battle of Vittorio Veneto, the
final coup de grâce was delivered in the last great
battle of World War I. Within days the Austro-
Hungarian empire dissolved and Italy made huge
territorial gains. Italian nationalists regard the battle
as a key milestone on the road to unification and
commemorations and information along the route
are well done and very interesting.

Follow the Piave east-southeast for 2.8km to a ro
bridge over the river, turn left and head into **Ponte de
Priulä** (70m).

The Hotel San Carlo (**www.hotelsancarlo.net**, tel 39
0438 27022) is located on the busy main street to the
north of the junction with an east-west road. It provides
bed and breakfast only but there are several restaurants
in the town.

STAGE 28
Ponte della Priulä to Bocca Callalta

Start	Hotel San Carlo, Ponte della Priulä (70m)
Distance	26km; from Susegana: 30km
Ascent/Descent	40m/110m
Difficulty	Easy
Walking time	6hr 10min; from Susegana: 7hr 10min
Maximum altitude	70m
Refreshments	There are surprisingly few places to stop for refreshments on the route but there is one particulary good place near Maserada sul Piave, about halfway. The Osteria, named Al Glorioso Piave, serves wonderful meals but will make a sandwich is something quicker is preferred.
Routefinding	Waymarking is limited but with care at the junctions it's an easy route to follow.

For the next 40km, all the way to Musile di Piave, the route follows the River
Piave across a flat landscape southeast.

There are two overnight options, the first at San Bartolomeo and the
second at Bocca Callalta. Both offer good accommodation but the preferred
option makes the next day, to Jesolo, eight rather than nine hours long.

Head south-southwest from Ponte della Priulä along t
main street and over the road bridge across the riv

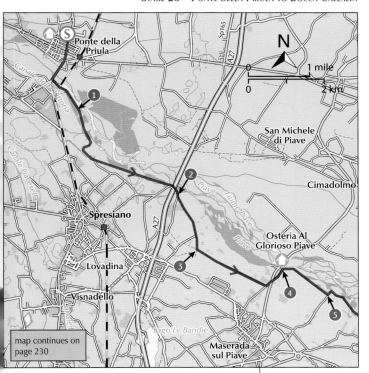

map continues on
page 230

Follow a track east below the levée and pass under the railway bridge. After 1.7km the track, now passing through an area of birch trees and shrubs, swings south-west and follows a dirt road through a gravel works (**1**). Emerging after about 300m head southeast and then east along a path on top of a low levée for 2.8km, then pass under a motorway. Next to the path is a strange collection of World War I memorabilia, possibly an informal war memorial.

From an **agricultural perspective** there is plenty to see – enormously tall crops of maize, beans

229

A field of (possibly flageolet!) beans

(flageolet, I think) and, of course, vineyards. Prosecco is produced here in industrial quantities and if you're on the route in early September watch out for harvesting machines and tractors pulling trailers loaded with lime green grapes hurtling down the tiny lanes. The wine, drunk over lunch and at the end of a hot day, is lovely stuff and very cheap.

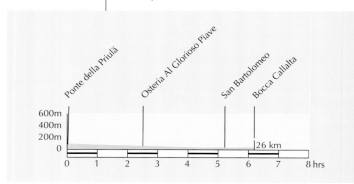

230

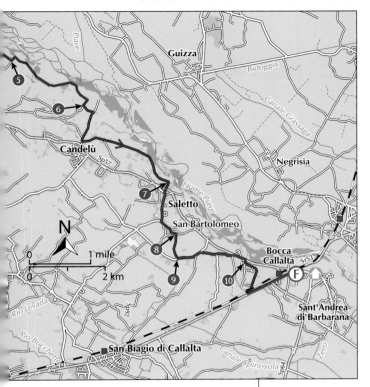

Turn right on the other side of the motorway and ollow a dirt road (**2**) south-southeast for 1.9km. At a unction turn left onto another dirt road (**3**) going east r 2.5km to a junction with metalled road. You are now the southern outskirts of **Maserada sul Piave**. Turn left the junction and head northeast to a junction with a ajor road – cross it and continue northeast. The **Osteria Glorioso Piave** is 200m further on, on the left.

The Traumpfad visits various sites which commem- orate the final battle of World War I, the **Battle of**

Vittorio Veneto, including one near the Osteria Al Glorioso Piave explaining the crucial role played by the Gordon Highlanders who were part of the British contingent shipped out to Italy for the last 18 months of the war.

Continue from the Osteria and turn east (**4**) as the road reaches the river. After 300m along the road join a path and continue southeast for 1.2km to a junction with a small local road (**5**). Turn left and then right after 200m and follow an access road southeast for 2.2km. Follow the road that swings sharply southwest before turning east again after 200m reaching a junction after 300m. Turn right (**6**) and follow the road south towards **Candelù**.

As the road enters the village take the first left (do not go as far as the main road) onto another road going east then south (**7**) to Saletto. Head south through **Saletto**, across the main road, past the church and out of the village. Continue south for 500m, turn left at a junction with a larger road and head into the centre of **San Bartolomeo**.

San Bartolomeo has a modern hotel, the Hotel Columbo (**www.hotel-colombo.it**, tel 39 0422 686685) in the centre of town. Even if you're not staying it's a good place for afternoon ice cream.

Following the main road through town continue east past the church. After 50m (**8**) turn right and south along the Via 12 Octobre turning left onto the Via Indipendenza after 700m (**9**). Continue northeast for 600m to a junction and then turn right and east and continue east to a junction with a busy road 1km later.

The **quickest way to the hotel** is to turn right at the junction and follow the road east for 1.6km to Bocca Callalta. It is, however, an unpleasant, possibly dangerous walk as there is little by way of a footpath and the traffic is fast moving.

Stay on the right-hand side of the road and then turn right (**10**) after 300m and then take the first left along the Via Gabriele D'Appunzio. Follow the road east and then southeast and underneath a railway line to the main road. Turn left onto the pavement and head northeast.

On the left is **Museo Soldati della Battaglia**, built in 1932 (typical of modernist Italian Facist architecture) and a little further along and on the right is the Albergo Callalta.

The Albergo Callalta (**www.albergocallalta.it**, tel 39 0422 895715) is a modest, good value hotel and extremely popular with locals who rate its pizzas very highly.

STAGE 29
Bocca Callalta to Jesolo

Start	Albergo Callalta, Bocca Callalta (10m)
Distance	31km
Ascent/Descent	60m/70m
Difficulty	Easy
Walking time	8hr
Maximum altitude	10m
Refreshments	At Musile di Paive

For the first half of the day the route continues its journey along the top of levées and visits a series of World War I locations along the way. After four hours it reaches Musile di Paive, almost exactly half way to Jesolo. This is quite a large town with plenty of facilities and it's worth stopping here as there is a lot of road walking in the second half of the stage, which will be hard work if it's hot. The roads are thankfully empty and run through marshland just to the north of the Laguna Veneta.

Jesolo has a huge church tower that can be seen from a great distance and gets closer slowly. In the past there was a German Beer Garden that provided respite about 6km from the town but unfortunately there were not enough Germans to keep it going. All that's left are the signs, and there is now no option but to slog on to Jesolo.

Note that Jesolo is not the same place as Lido de Jesolo, the beach resort that runs along the long sand spit that separates Laguna Veneta from the Adriatic. That resort has hundreds of hotels – Jesolo has only two.

From the hotel in Bocca Callalta head northeast alon the main road, turn right after 50m and follow a quie road running east then southeast along the top of a levée As the road passes above the last houses in the village swings east and heads off into the distance. Stay on th road for nearly 3km then turn right (**1**) following a sma road down to a larger one. Turn left at the junction wit the main road and follow it into **Zenson di Piave** wher there are a range of services including cafes.

Continue along the main road southeast out of tow and as the road swings south (**2**) climb up onto the levé and follow a grassy path southeast. After 1.8km, as th levée starts to swing southeast (**3**), turn right along a pa and descend down to a road. Turn left onto the roa follow it southeast 1.4km (crossing a motorway over bridge) and take a path (**4**) that climbs onto a small road (the original road continues on into Fossalta Piave). Continue southeast along the road, cross a ro after 300m (which heads down to a bridge over th Piave) and continue southeast along a dirt track.

Fossalta di Piave is where **Ernest Hemingway** was posted as a Red Cross ambulance driver for a few weeks in 1918 and wounded. The experience provided the inspiration for *A Farewell to Arms* the book that secured Hemingway's reputation. Although Hemingway was not in action for as long as the hero of the book he did get wounded and, like the novel's protagonist, fell in love with his nurse.

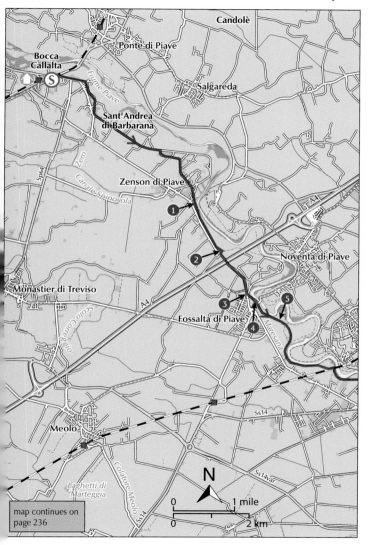

map continues on page 236

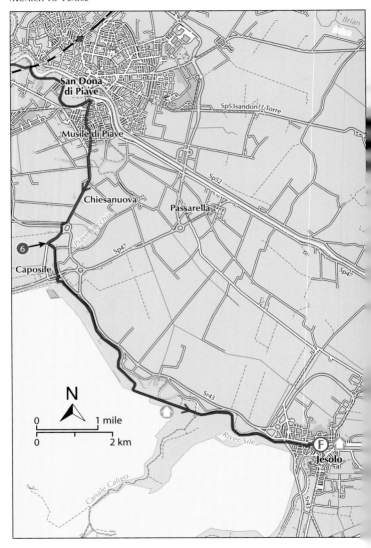

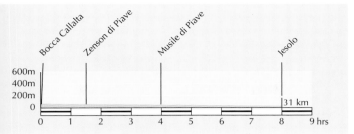

Continue east-southeast along the levée. After a kilometre take a right hand fork (**5**) and follow the top of the levée as it swings south (cutting off in the river). After 600m the tracks reunite and the route follows the river swinging southeast. Ignore a right hand turn after 200m and continue with the river along a grassy path with trees to the left and fields to the right. Cutting across another meander the levée crosses a field and reaches a railway line. Here the path is a little obscure but stay on the north side of the line and head down to the river to join footpath and follow it and the river underneath the railway line. ▶

The footpath is now in mature trees.

After a few metres turn right onto a well-defined path and follow it once more to the top of the levée and turn left. Continue along path emerging from the trees from path across (above) farmland with the river now at some distance. Eventually the path swings east to Musile di Piave. Stay on the levée to the bridge over the river if you want to see an incredibly heroic war memorial; otherwise save time, drop down to the road, cut off the corner and head into town.

Musile di Piave is quite a large town with the full range of services including, if needed, accommodation at the Hotel Calaluna (**www.hotel-calaluna. com/it**, tel 39 0421 53303). It was completely destroyed in World War I and rebuilt in the 1920s. As the next part of the walk is nearly all on a road it's a good place to stop and recharge the batteries for the ordeal ahead.

Memorial at Musile di Piave

Head south on the main street (initially the Via Ror and then the Via Martin) out of town to a roundabou Cross the roundabout and follow a tree-lined road sou for 2km. As the road approaches another roundabo turn right along an access road and then, after 50m, l following an underpass beneath a larger road. Contin south to a junction with a road and follow it southwe through scattered houses. At the edge of the settleme (**6**) turn left and head east past farm buildings on a d track. After 300m turn right at a junction and go sou After 900m alongside a dirt road emerge onto a ma road with a prosecco factory to the right.

You have now arrived at the small village of Caposile, the last place for refreshments before a final 10km and 2hr 30min slog to Jesolo. There is also a bed and break-fast there, the L'Erba Matta (**www.erbamatta.it**, tel 38 0421 230 397.

Cross the main road, still following the river, a continue south along a small access road to a junctic

ere you turn right. After a few metres turn left down to
River Sile and over a pontoon bridge dating back to
World War II. ▶ Turn left on the other side and follow
oad east then southeast.

> Walkers don't have to pay a toll to cross the bridge.

The routes follows a road across a slip of marshy
land between the River Sile to the northeast and the
Laguna di Venezia. These **wetlands**, which feature
along the coast all the way to Trieste are important
for wildlife, particularly birds and fish, and there
are many reserves. Expect to see herons, egrets and
kingfishers skimming across still water.

The route follows a virtually empty road that runs
utheast of the River Sile and immediately northeast of
e Laguna di Venezia. Follow it for 9.5km all the way
Jesolo.

Jesolo has two hotels, the Hotel Udinese da Aldo
(**www.daaldo.com**, tel 39 0421 951407) which is
good value but basic. The Al Ponte de Fero (**www.
alpontedefero.it**, tel 39 0421 350785), on the seaward
road east of the main town centre, is a boutique hotel
with excellent food. An alternative reached about 2km
before Jesola is the Country House Salomè which pro-
duces its own wine.

STAGE 30

Jesolo to Venice

Start	Town square, Jesolo (2m)
Distance	23km
Ascent/Descent	negligible
Difficulty	Easy
Walking time	6hr
Maximum altitude	na

If you're an experienced long-distance walker you may be familiar with an end of walk anti-climax. After a simple daily routine the mind inevitably starts to think about a more complicated life that waits back home. Venice however is the perfect antidote. What a destination – can anywhere else in world to compare with the amazing combination of water, colour and light? When Samuel Johnson famously wrote 'when a man is tired of London, he is tired of life' he should have been talking about Venice.

The slog across the Venetian plain has now been completed but there is still six hours of walking before the ferry and Venice. The pleasant first part, avoiding the flesh pots of the Lido di Jesolo, follows the west side of the sand spit that divides the Adriatic from the Laguna di Venezia along the banks of the River Sile to the Ponte Cavallino. The second part is a roadside slog redeemed only by the opportunity to pose in the Adriatic near the end.

The ferry terminal marks the finish point – 569km north to south across the Alps – but the short voyage past the Lido di Venezia into the gorgeous bustling heart of Venice at Piazza San Marco completes the journey.

From the town square (Piazza Donatori del Sangue) st[...] ing on the northern or left-hand side of the river, foll[...] the riverside Via Nazario Sauro south. As the river mea[...] ders west, stick with it, leave the main road (**1**) and foll[...] the Via Riveria Sile. When the metalled road finishes lea[...] it and follow a grassy path that swings south with the ri[...]

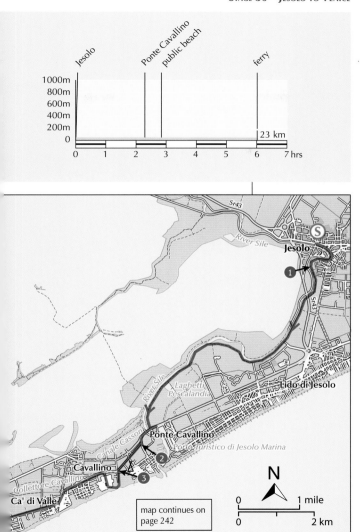

map continues on
page 242

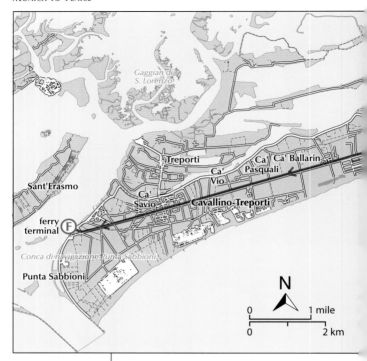

right). The path sticks limpet like to the river for the ne
9km.

> Although the path goes through a **nature reserve**
> the classic Adriatic wetlands are on the other side
> of the river. Judging by the number of people trying
> to catch them it must be full of fish. There is even
> an example of a 'Chinese fishing net' a fixed instal-
> lation where a huge net at the end of a long lever is
> lowered from land into the water. Birdlife along this
> stretch is particularly rich.

Chinese fishing net on the Fiume Sile

After 9km you reach **Ponte Cavallino** – a busy road ridge that has to be crossed. After a short walk along the main road (perhaps after stopping for refreshments at the ar on the corner), take the first left (**2**) and then the first ght and follow a quiet road southwest for a kilometre. At junction (**3**) near a large campsite take a short path to a ublic beach. ▶

This is best spot for triumphant MV walkers celebrating crossing to Alps to pose for photographs with their feet in the Adriatic.

Having removed the sand from your toes and navi-ted back through the campsite turn left at the road. Go est for a kilometre, turn left at a roundabout (**4**) and ead into the centre of **Ca' di Valle** where there are plenty lunch options. From Ca' di Valle it's 10km alongside e Via Fuasta to a roundabout, car parks and the ferry Venice.

It's over – you've made it!

APPENDIX A
Route planner

Cumulative distances given assume that all A routes are taken within that section
H = Hotel/refuge; R = restaurant; B = bar; S = shop; ATM = cashpoint

Places with facilities	Facilities	Time	Cumulative time	Distance (km)	Cumulative distance
1 Munich to the Inn Valley					
Stage 1					
Munich	All services				
Pullach	R,B,S,ATM	1hr 30min	1hr 30min	12.7	12.7
Gaststätte Brückenwirt	R	10min	1hr 40min	.9	13.6
Kloster Schäftlarn	H,R,B	3hr 40min	5hr 20min	10.2	23.8
Gasthaus Brückenfischer	H,R,B	10min	5hr 30min	1	24.8
Wolfratshausen	All services	2hr 40min	8hr 10min	9.2	34
Stage 2					
Bad Tölz	All services	7hr 10min	15hr 20min	28	62
Stage 3					
Arzbach	R,B	1hr 40min	17hr	7	69
	All services	1hr	18hr	3.4	72.4

244

Places with facilities	Facilities	Time	Cumulative time	Distance (km)	Cumulative distance
Brauneck	R,B	10min	18hr 10min	1.3	73.7
Reiseralm	R,B	20min	18hr 30min	1	74.7
Brauneckhaus	H,R,B	1hr 30min	20hr	3.8	78.5
Tutzinger Hütte	H,R,B	3hr	23hr	4.5	83
Stage 4					
Jachenau	H,R,B	4hr	27hr	9	92
Vorderriß	H,R,B	3hr 20min	30hr 20min	9	101
Stage 5					
Oswaldhütte	R,B	50min	31hr 10min	6.3	107.3
Hinteriß	H,R,B	1hr 30min	32hr 40min	4.7	112
Karwendelhaus	H,R,B	4hr 50min	37hr 30min	13	125
Stage 6					
Kastenalm	R,B	6hr 30min	44hr	10	135
Hallerangerhaus	H,R,B	2hr 30min	46hr 30min	5	140
Stage 7A					
St Magdalena	R,B	2hr 50min	49hr 20min	6.7	146.7

Places with facilities	Facilities	Time	Cumulative time	Distance (km)	Cumulative distance
Hall	All services	1hr 40min	51hr	7.3	154
Stage 7B					
St Magdalena	R,B	2hr 50min	49hr 20min	6.7	
Gasthof Martinsstuben	H,R,B	1hr 40min	51hr	7.3	
Wattens	All services	1hr 40min	52hr 40min	5	
2 Inn Valley to Pfunders					
Stage 8A (from Hall)					
Tulfes	H,R,B	2hr 10min	2hr 10min	7	7
Gasthof Windegg	H,R,B	50min	3hr	2.7	9.7
Glückserhütte	R,B	50min	3hr 50min	1.3	11
Tulfein Alm	R,B	3hr	6hr 50min	7	18
Glungezer Hütte	H,R,B	2hr	8hr 50min	22	22
Stage 8B (from Wattens)					
Gasthof Mühle	R,B	2hr 50min	2hr 50min	10	
Gasthof Säge	H,R,B	10min	3hr	1	
Gasthof Haneburger	H,R,B	50min	3hr 50min	3	
Lizumer Hütte	H,R,B	3hr 50min	7hr 40min	3	

Places with Facilities	Facilities	Time	Cumulative time	Distance (km)	Cumulative distance
Stage 9					
Lizumer Hütte	H,R,B	8hr 40min	17hr 30min	15	37
Stage 10					
Tuxer Joch Huas	H,R,B	6hr 30min	24hr	10	47*
Stage 11A					
Friensenberghaus (just off the route)	H,R,B	4hr 20min	28hr 20min	7	54*
Olpererhütte	H,R,B	2hr 10min	30hr 30min	4	58*
Stage 11B					
Caraerhütte	H,R,B	4hr 40min		10	
Stage 12A					
Pfitscher Joch Haus	H,R,B	4hr	34hr 30min	10	68*
Stein	H,R,B	1hr 30min	36hr	3	71*
Stage 12B					
Pfitscher Joch Haus	H,R,B	6hr 40min		11	
Stein	H,R,B	1hr 30min		3	
Stage 13					
Pfunders	H,R,B, ATM	8hr 10min	44hr 10min	20	91*

247

Places with facilities	Facilities	Time	Cumulative time	Distance (km)	Cumulative distance
3 Pfunders to Alleghe					
Stage 14					
Vallarga	H,R,B	1hr 40min	1hr 40min	6.8	6.8
Niedervintl	All services	1hr 20min	3hr	3.4	10.2
Roner Hütte	H,R,B	3hr 20min	6hr 20min	7.8	18
Kreuzwiesen Alm	H,R,B	1hr 40min	8hr	6	24
Stage 15					
Maurerberghütte	H,R,B	5hr	13hr	11.5	35.5
Würzjoch	H,R,B	1hr 30min	14hr 30min	4	39.5
Schlüterhütte	H,R,B	2hr	16hr 30min	6.5	46
Stage 16					
Medalgesalm	H,R,B	40min	17hr 10min	3	49
Puezhütte	H,R,B	4hr 20min	21hr 30min	8	57
Stage 17					
Grodner Joch	H,R,B	2hr 40min	24hr 10min	7.8	64.8
Rifugio Pisciadù	H,R,B	1hr 50min	26hr	2.2	67
Rifugio Boè	H R B	2hr 20min	28hr 20min	4	71

	Facilities	Time	Cumulative time	Distance (km)	Cumulative distance
Rifugio Capanna Fassa	H,R,B	2hr 20min	30hr 40min	0	71
Stage 18					
Rifugio Forcella Pordoi	H,R,B	40min	31hr 20min	2.3	73.3
Pordoi Joch	H,R,B	1hr 50min	32hr 10min	2	75.3
Rifugio Fredarola	H,R,B	30min	32hr 40min	1.4	76.7
Rifugio Viel dal Pan	H,R,B	1hr	33hr 40min	2.3	79
Stage 19					
Rifugio Castiglioni	H,R,B	1hr 30min	35hr 10min	4	83
Refugio Fedaia	H,R,B	30min	35hr 40min	3	86
Rifugio Capanna Bill di Darman	H,R,B	10min	35hr 50min	.7	86.7
Malga Ciapela	H,R,B	40min	36hr 30min	4.8	91.5
Sottoguda	H,R,B, ATM	40min	37hr 10min	2	93.5
Alleghe	All services	2hr 20min	39hr 30min	9.5	103
4 Alleghe to Belluno					
Stage 20					
Rifugio Coldai	H,R,B	4hr 20min	4hr 20min	8.6	8.6
Rifugio Tissi	H,R,B	1hr 50min	6hr 10min	4.4	13

Places with facilities	Facilities	Time	Cumulative time	Distance (km)	Cumulative distance
Stage 21					
Rifugio Vazzoler	H,R,B	1hr 40min	7hr 50min	6.5	19.5
Rifugio Bruto Carestiato	H,R,B	4hr 20min	12hr 10min	9.5	29
Stage 22					
Passo Duran	H,R,B	40min	12hr 50min	2.8	31.8
Rifugio Sommariva al Pramperet	H,R,B	4hr 20min	17hr 10min	10.7	42.5
Refugio Pian de Fontana	H,R,B	3hr	20hr 10min	6.5	49
Stage 23A					
Refugio 7th Alpini	H,R,B	8hr	28hr 10min	14	63
Stage 23B					
Rifugio Furio Bianchet	H,R,B	2hr 40min		4.5	
Stage 24					
Belluno	All services	4hr 20min	32hr 30min	14	77*
5 Belluno to Venice					
Stage 25					
Nevega	H,R,B	3hr 20min	3hr 20min	11	11
Rifugio Col Visentin	H,R,B	2hr 10min	5hr 30min	6	17

Places with facilities	Facilities	Time	Cumulative time	Distance (km)	Cumulative distance
Stage 26					
Rifugio Pian de le Femene	H,R,B	2hr 20min	7hr 50min	9	26
Revine	H,R,B	1hr 40min	9hr 30min	3	29
Nagorola	H,R,B	40min	10hr 10min	2.5	31.5
Tarzo	H,R,B, ATM	1hr	11hr 10min	3.5	35
Stage 27					
Refrontolo	H,R,B	2hr 30min	13hr 40min	10.7	45.7
Collato	H,R,B	2hr	15hr 40min	8.9	54.6
Susegana option	H,R,B, ATM			3.4	58
Ponte della Priula	All services	1hr 50min	17hr 30min	6	64
Stage 28					
Osteria Al Glorioso Piave	H,R,B	2hr 30min	20hr	13	77
San Bartolomeo	All services	2hr 40min	22hr 40min	8	85
Bocca Callalta	H,R,B	1hr	23hr 40min	5	90
Stage 29					
Zenson di Piave	All services	1hr 30min	25hr 10min	5.9	95.9
Fossalta di Piave	R,B	50min	26hr	3.7	99.6

Places with facilities	Facilities	Time	Cumulative time	Distance (km)	Cumulative distance
Musile di Piave	All services	1hr 40min	27hr 40min	5.9	105.5
Caposile	H,R,B	1hr 10min	28hr 50min	5.7	111.2
Jesolo	All services	3hr 50min	32hr 40min	9.8	121
Stage 30					
Ponte Cavallino	R.B	2hr 20min	35hr	9.3	130.3
Ferry to Venice		3hr 40min	38hr 40min	13.7	144

APPENDIX B

Facilities along the route

ction 1

oster Schäftlarn
osterbräu Stüberl
ww.klosterbraeustueberl-schaeftlarn.de
49 8178 3694

sthaus Brückenfischer
ww.bruckenfischer.de
49 8178 3635

olfratshausen
sthof Humpbräu
ww.humplbraeu.de
49 8171 483290

tel Isartaler Hof
ww.hotel-isartaler-hof.de
49 8171 2388122

d Tölz
tel Kolbergarten
ww.hotel-kolbergarten.de
49 8041 78920

sthotel Kolberbräu
ww.kolberbraeu.de
49 8041 76880

nggries
tel Altwirt
ww.altwirt-lenggries.de
49 8042 97320

sthof Pension Neuwirt
ww.neuwirt.info
49 8042 8943

auneckhaus
ww.brauneckgipfelhaus.de
49 8042 8786

Tutzinger Hütte
www.dav-tutzinger-huette.de
Tel 49 0175 1641690 (mobile)

Jachenau
Gasthof zur Jachenau
www.hotel-gasthof-jachenau-toelzer-
land.de
Tel 49 8043 910
(closed on Tuesdays)

Vorderriß
Gasthof Post
www.post-vorderriss.de
Tel 49 80 45277

Hinteriß
Hotel Gasthof zur Post
www.post-hinteriss.info
Tel 43 5245 206

Karwendelhaus
www.karwendelhaus.com
Tel 43 720 983554

Hallerangerhaus
The Hallerangerhaus
www.hallerangerhaus.at
Tel 43 72034 7028

Halleranger Alm
www.halleranger-alm.at
Tel 43 664 1055955

Hall
Goldener Engl
www.goldener-engl.at
Tel 43 5223 54 6 21

Gasthof Badl
www.badl.at/en
Tel 43 5223 56784

Gasthof Martinsstuben
www.martinsstuben.at
Tel 43 5223 52501

Wattens
Hotel Goldener Adler
www.goldener-adler-wattens.at
Tel 43 5224 52255

Pension Clara
www.pension-clara.at
Tel 43 5224 52151

Section 2

Tulfes
Hotel Pension Glungezer
www.glungezer.net
Tel 43 5223 78302

Gasthof Neuwirt
www.neuwirt-tulfes.at
Tel 43 5223 78309

Gasthof Windegg
Tel 43 5223 78313

Glungezer Hütte
www.glungezer.at
Tel 43 5223 78018

Gasthof Säge
Tel 43 5224 53173

Gasthof Haneburger
Tel 43 5224 53875

Lizumer Hütte
www.glungezer.at
Tel 43 664 647 5353

Tuxer Joch Haus
www.tuxerjochhaus.at
Tel 43 5287 87216
(no reservations by phone)

Friensenberghaus
(just off the route)
www.friesenberghaus.com
Tel 43 676 7497550

Olpererhütte
www.olpererhuette.de
Tel 43 664 4176566 (mobile)

Geraerhütte
www.geraerhuette.at
Tel 43 676 9610 303

Pfitscher Joch Haus
www.pfitscherjochhaus.com
Tel 39 472 630119

Stein
Gasthof Stein
Tel 39 472 630 130

Pfunders
Gasthof Brugge
www.gasthof-brugger.com
Tel 39 0472 549 155

Vallarga
Haus Gitschberg
www.haus-gitschberg.com
Tel 39 472 548057

Niedervintl
Lodenwirt
www.lodenwirt.com
Tel 39 472 867000

Roner Hütte
www.ronerhuette.it
Tel 39 472 546016

Section 3

Kreuzwiesen Alm
www.kreuzwiesenalm.com
Tel 39 472 413 714

Maurerberghütte
www.maurerberg.com
Tel 39 474 520059

Würzjoch
www.wuerzjoch.com
Tel 39 0474 52 00 66

Schlütterhütte
www.schlueterhuette.com
Tel 39 0472 670072

Medalgesalm
www.medalges.com
Tel 39 347 5049169

Puezhütte
www.rifugiopuez.it
Tel 39 0471 795 365

Grodner Joch

Rifugio Fraro
the sign on the building is Refugio
Alpino)
www.rifugiofrara.it
Tel 39 0471 795225

Hotel Cir
www.hotelcir.com
Tel 39 0471 795127

Rifugio Pisciadù
Tel 39 471 836292

Rifugio Boè
www.rifugioboe.it
Tel 39 0471 847303

Rifugio Capanna Fassa
www.rifugiocapannafassa.com
Tel 39 3385 4736 24
Tel 39 0462 601723

Rifugio Forcella Pordoi
Tel 39 368 355 7505

Pordoi Joch

Hotel Savoia
www.savoiahotel.net
Tel 39 462 601717

Rifugio Fredarola
www.fredarola.it
Tel 39 462 602072

Rifugio Viel dal Pan
www.rifugiovieldalpan.com
Tel 39 339 3865241

Rifugio Castiglioni
www.rifugiomarmolada.it
Tel 39 0462 601117

Refugio Fedaia
www.rifugiofedaia.com
Tel 39 437 0722007

Rifugio Capanna Bill di Darman
www.capannabill.com
Tel 39 0437 722100

Sottoguda

Hotel La Montanara
www.lamontanara.it
Tel 39 0437 722017

Hotel Garni Al Serrai
www.aiserrai.com
Tel 04 3772 2120

Alleghe

Sport Hotel Europa
sporthoteleuropa.com
Tel 39 04 3752 3362

Hotel Central Alleghe
www.hotelcentralalleghe.com
Tel 39 0437 523476

Section 4
Rifugio Coldai
Tel 39 0473 789160

Rifugio Tissi
Tel 39 0437 721644

Rifugio Vazzoler
Tel 39 0437 660008

Rifugio Bruto Carestiato
www.rifugiocarestiato.com
Tel 39 0437-62949

Passo Duran
Refugio San Sebastiano
www.passoduran.it
Tel 37 0437 62360

Refugio Passo Duran
www.rifugiopassoduran.it
Tel 39 3464 165461

Rifugio Sommariva al Pramperet
www.rifugiosommarivaalpramperet.it
Tel 39 437 1956153

Refugio Pian de Fontana
Tel 39 335 609 6819

Refugio 7th Alpini
www.rifugiosettimoalpini.com
Tel 39 437 94 16 31

Rifugio Furio Bianchet
Tel 39 335 644 6975

Belluno
Casa per Ferie 'Al Centro'
www.centrocongressibelluno.it/casa.
html
Tel 39 437 944 460

Albergo Cappello
www.albergocappello.com
Tel 39 437 940246

Section 5
Rifugio Col Visentin
www.rifugiocolvisentin.net
Tel 39 0437 27110

Rifugio Pian de le Femene
Tel 39 0438 583645

Revine
Ai Cadelach Hotel Ristorante Benessere
www.cadelach.it
Tel 39 0438 523010

Nagorola
La Nicchia
Tel 39 0438 524098

Tarzo
Albergo Ai Pini
www.albergoaipini.it
Tel 39 04 3858 6206

Susegana
Hotel Astoria
www.hotel-astoria.com
Tel 39 0438 738525

Ponte della Priula
Hotel San Carlo
www.hotelsancarlo.net
Tel 39 0438 27022

San Bartolomeo
Hotel Columbo
www.hotel-colombo.it
Tel 39 0422 686685

Bocca Callalta
Albergo Callalta
www.albergocallalta.it
Tel 39 0422 895715

Musile di Piave
Hotel Calaluna
www.hotel-calaluna.com/it
Tel 39 0421 53303

Caposile
L'Erba Matta
www.erbamatta.it
Tel 39 0421 230 397

Jesolo
Hotel Udinese da Aldo
www.daaldo.com
Tel 39 0421 951407

Al Ponte de Fero
www.alpontedefero.it
Tel 39 0421350785

(2km before the town)
Country House Salomè
www.countryhousesalome.it
Tel 39 0421 230528

APPENDIX C
Useful contacts

Walking Information

The Austrian Alpine Club website
www.alpenverein.at
An excellent source of information and includes all you need to know about finding and staying in a hut, with links via the 'hüttenfinder' to individual hut websites or pages on the site. It's worth checking the site as you plan your trip as the approach to booking is developing all the time. The individual hut websites typically include information on the local network of routes and how long it takes to get from one hut to another.

Alpine Club Membership
For discounts in the huts, mountain insurance and other benefits. British citizens can join the British Section.
www.aacuk.org.uk

Maps and Navigation

GPS
www.viewranger.com
The Viewranger GPS app runs on Apple and Android smartphones and maps can be purchased in their online store.

Printed maps
The Map Shop
15 High Street
Upton-upon-Severn
WR8 0HJ
www.themapshop.co.uk

Stanfords
12-14 Long Acre
London
WC2E 9LP
www.standfords.co.uk

Transport

Air
Situated right in the middle of Europe the walk is easy to get to. Munich Airport is an important international airport, the second biggest in Germany and the seventh in Europe. Although not quite as big, Venice Marco Polo Airport has connections to most major European cities and some long haul destinations in the US and Middle East.
Easyjet
www.easyjet.com

Ryanair
www.ryanair.com

Rail
Germany - Deutsche Bahn (DB)
www.bahn.com

Austria - Österreichische Bundesbahne (OBB)
www.oebb.at

Italy – Trenitalia
www.trenitalia.com

For advice on rail travel go to
www.seat61.com

us/coach

Italy and the Dolomites bus/coach
avel is particularly relevant – the most
nportant operator is Dolomiti Bus –
ww.dolomitibus.it

or multimode transport planning
om anywhere to anywhere then try
ww.rome2rio.com. Although the
formation provided is not completely
liable it is a good starting point.

Emergencies and Health
In the mountains mobile phone
coverage is patchy. If you can get a
connection, help should be available
in English on the European emergency
number 112. Alpine club membership
(see above) includes policy cover for
high altitude walking but if you're a UK
resident and carrying a European Health
Insurance Card (EHIC) you should be
able to get free health care.

DOWNLOAD THE ROUTE
IN GPX FORMAT

All the routes in this guide are available for download from:

www.cicerone.co.uk/804/GPX

as GPX files. You should be able to load them into most formats of mobile device, whether GPS or smartphone.

When you go to this link, you will be asked for your email address and where you purchased the guide, and have the option to subscribe to the Cicerone e-newsletter.

www.cicerone.co.uk

LISTING OF CICERONE GUIDES

Short Walks in Lakeland
  1 South Lakeland
  2 North Lakeland
  3 West Lakeland
The Cumbria Coastal Way
The Cumbria Way
Tour of the Lake District

DERBYSHIRE, PEAK DISTRICT AND MIDLANDS

High Peak Walks
Scrambles in the Dark Peak
The Star Family Walks
Walking in Derbyshire
White Peak Walks
  The Northern Dales
  The Southern Dales

SOUTHERN ENGLAND

Suffolk Coast & Heaths Walks
The Cotswold Way
The Great Stones Way
The Kennet and Avon Canal
The Lea Valley Walk
The North Downs Way
The Peddars Way and Norfolk
  Coast Path
The Ridgeway National Trail
The South Downs Way
The South West Coast Path
The Thames Path
The Two Moors Way
Walking in Cornwall
Walking in Essex
Walking in Kent
Walking in Norfolk
Walking in Sussex
Walking in the Chilterns
Walking in the Cotswolds
Walking in the Isles of Scilly
Walking in the New Forest
Walking in the North
  Wessex Downs
Walking in the Thames Valley
Walking on Dartmoor
Walking on Guernsey
Walking on Jersey
Walking on the Isle of Wight
Walking the Jurassic Coast
Walks in the South Downs
  National Park

WALES AND WELSH BORDERS

Glyndwr's Way
Great Mountain Days
  in Snowdonia
Hillwalking in Snowdonia
Hillwalking in Wales: 1&2
Mountain Walking in Snowdonia

Offa's Dyke Path
Ridges of Snowdonia
Scrambles in Snowdonia
The Ascent of Snowdon
The Ceredigion and Snowdonia
  Coast Paths
The Lleyn Peninsula Coastal Path
The Pembrokeshire Coastal Path
The Severn Way
The Shropshire Hills
The Wales Coast Path
The Wye Valley Walk
Walking in Carmarthenshire
Walking in Pembrokeshire
Walking in the Forest of Dean
Walking in the South Wales
  Valleys
Walking in the Wye Valley
Walking on the Brecon Beacons
Walking on the Gower
Welsh Winter Climbs

INTERNATIONAL CHALLENGES, COLLECTIONS AND ACTIVITIES

Canyoning in the Alps
Europe's High Points
The Via Francigena: 1&2

EUROPEAN CYCLING

Cycle Touring in France
Cycle Touring in Spain
Cycle Touring in Switzerland
Cycling in the French Alps
Cycling the Canal du Midi
Cycling the River Loire
The Danube Cycleway: 1&2
The Grand Traverse of the
  Massif Central
The Moselle Cycle Route
The Rhine Cycle Route
The Way of St James

AFRICA

Climbing in the Moroccan
  Anti-Atlas
Kilimanjaro
Mountaineering in the Moroccan
  High Atlas
The High Atlas
Trekking in the Atlas Mountains
Walking in the Drakensberg

ALPS – CROSS-BORDER ROUTES

100 Hut Walks in the Alps
Across the Eastern Alps: E5
Alpine Points of View
Alpine Ski Mountaineering
  1 Western Alps

Chamonix to Zermatt
The Tour of the Bernina
Tour of Mont Blanc
Tour of Monte Rosa
Tour of the Matterhorn
Trail Running – Chamonix and
  the Mont Blanc region
Trekking in the Alps
Trekking in the Silvretta and
  Rätikon Alps
Walking in the Alps
Walks and Treks in the
  Maritime Alps

PYRENEES AND FRANCE/ SPAIN CROSS-BORDER ROUTES

The GR10 Trail
The GR11 Trail – La Senda
The Mountains of Andorra
The Pyrenean Haute Route
The Pyrenees
The Way of St James:
  France & Spain
Walks and Climbs in the Pyren

AUSTRIA

The Adlerweg
Trekking in Austria's Hohe Tau
Trekking in the Stubai Alps
Trekking in the Zillertal Alps
Walking in Austria

BELGIUM AND LUXEMBOURG

Walking in the Ardennes

EASTERN EUROPE

The High Tatras
The Mountains of Romania
Walking in Bulgaria's
  National Parks
Walking in Hungary

FRANCE

Chamonix Mountain Adventur
Ecrins National Park
Mont Blanc Walks
Mountain Adventures in
  the Maurienne
The Cathar Way
The GR20 Corsica
The GR5 Trail
The Robert Louis Stevenson Tr
Tour of the Oisans: The GR54
Tour of the Queyras
Tour of the Vanoise
Vanoise Ski Touring
Via Ferratas of the French Alps
Walking in Corsica

Walking – Trekking – Mountaineering – Climbing – Cycling

Over 40 years, Cicerone have built up an outstanding collection of over 300 guides, inspiring all sorts of amazing adventures.

Every guide comes from extensive exploration and research by our expert authors, all with a passion for their subjects. They are frequently praised, endorsed and used by clubs, instructors and outdoor organisations.

All our titles can now be bought as **e-books**, **ePubs** and **Kindle** files and we also have an online magazine – **Cicerone Extra** – with features to help cyclists, climbers, walkers and trekkers choose their next adventure, at home or abroad.

Our website shows any **new information** we've had in since a book was published. Please do let us know if you find anything has changed, so that we can publish the latest details. On our **website** you'll also find great ideas and lots of detailed information about what's inside every guide and you can buy **individual routes** from many of them online.

It's easy to keep in touch with what's going on at Cicerone by getting our monthly **free e-newsletter**, which is full of offers, competitions, up-to-date information and topical articles. You can subscribe on our home page and also follow us on **Facebook** and **Twitter** or dip into our **blog**.

Cicerone – the very best guides for exploring the world.

CICERONE

2 Police Square Milnthorpe Cumbria LA7 7PY
Tel: 015395 62069 info@cicerone.co.uk
www.cicerone.co.uk and **www.cicerone-extra.com**